**I dedicate this book to my family and friends.
God bless you all!**

In memory of my father and grandparents.

You Can't do that! Yes I Can!
Copyright © 2017 by Michael Attardi

All rights reserved. No part of this book may be reproduced or transmitted in any form or
by any means without written permission from the author. All content and photos owned
by Michael Attardi.

ISBN: 978-0-9777838-5-4
Printed in USA by Amazon

Table of Contents

ACT III

Acknowledgements

Like the driftwood on my cover, it's considered to be dead wood floating upon the ocean without purpose until it lands on the shore. Someone finds it and gives it a new life. Never will it be found without someone recognizing its potential.

I want to acknowledge all those that were instrumental in my personal life and my professional career. I have been blessed to have met so many people who have helped me on my journey to create an everlasting legacy. I am very thankful to the following individuals who have influenced, coached, and inspired me on the different paths that I have traveled. Some of you may not know how much you have helped play a huge role in my life. THANK YOU FOR BEING THERE!

Gentry Akens, Marcus Allen, Dominic Ambrosio, Joe Anselmo, John Avalone, O.J. Anderson, Stan "Chip" Albers, Dr. Michael Arvanitis, Dr. Harry Bade, Matt Baker, Coach George Baldwin, Bob Biasi, Senator Bill Bradley, Tim Brown, Senator Lloyd Benson, Tony Bennett, Trish Bleier, Stephanie Bowman, Carol Burnett, Jay Brower, Michael Broggie, Sharon Broggie, Dean Blandino, Coach Rich Braun, Jim Belushi, Vincent Borelli,

Terell Canton, Kim Carroll, Raul Ceide, David Ciambrone, George Conti, Donna Clay, Patrick Clay, Marc Clayton, Vinny Correa, Roger Craig, Tim Curry, Tony Curtis, Jim Daopoulos, Darryl Dawkins, Al Davis, Marc Davis, Robert DeNiro, Joe DiMaggio, Roy Patrick Disney, Dani Donaldi, Bryan Ecochardt, Keith Elias, Roy Ellison, Grayson Everidge, Joseph Ferraina, Jerry Fernicola, Michael Feinstein, Vincent Fiore, Harry Flattery, Larry Florida,

James Gandolfini, Jason Garrett, Jim Garrett, John Garrett, Judd Garrett, Ralph Garry, Bill George, Roger Goodell, Elvis Gooden Sr., John Hadity, Uta Hagen, Tom Hanks, Nolan Harrison, Jim Hart, Richard Cole-Hatchard, Sandra Cole-Hatchard, Brian Henson, Kenny Hill, Mike Hollis, Wally Hough, Gene Huber, Marcia Hurwitz, Magic Johnson, Ollie Johnston, Ron Jaworski, Tim Kane, Ward Kimball, Senator Edward Kennedy,

Congressman Joseph P. Kennedy, Larry Little, Skip Longenberger, George Lopez, Coach Jack Levy, Chief Dave Ogden, Steve M. Marylee Ortamayer, Grand Master Mac Dom, Mickey Mantle, Dan Marino, Jerry Markbreit, Tess Marsalis, Nick Massaro, Phil

Maui, Seneca McMillan, Tony Michalek, Sam Mills, Liza Minnelli,

Greg Montgomery, Earl & Jane Morrall, Alan Moss, John Nies, Monica Nordell, Steve Ortmeyer, Congressman Frank Pallone, Chazz Palminteri, Bill Parcells, Eric Peduto, James Perri, Luke Perry, Evgeny Platov, Kim Praniewicz, Coach Ed Ray, Andre Reed, Keanu Reeves, Andre Roca, Mickey Rourke, Chico Rouse Jr, Joe Sansone,

Alan Schneider, Kenny Schwartz, Carlos Sciortino, Lars Schilling, Pat Scire, Coach George Silk, Chris Smith, Steven Sondheim, Pete Stenonovich, Michael Strahan, Paul "Kit" Stolen, Danny Stubbs, Joe Theisman, Frank Thomas, Gladstone Trott, Henry Vaccarro, Andy Van Roon, Phil Villapiano, Paul Zambrano.

Colleen and I wanted to thank all our friends.

Colleen and I have been so blessed to have so many incredible friends in our lives. They are friends that are all special to us. If we do not see them for months, we pick up where we left off like no time had passed. Charlesy and Tommy Cornejo, Evgeny and Jeaneen Platov, Rebecca and Wes Bohen, Alan and Rue Schneider, Reshi and Nalini Mohamed, Sean and Shea Bradley, Thom and Brenda Huff, Todd and Michelle Chase, Eric and Stephanie Peduto, Ralph and Sandra Garry, Bryan and Michele Ecochardt, Dr. Chris and Stephanie Cortman, Vinnie Fiore, George Curvy, Tony Racioppi, Doug Dunn, Lou Morreale, Carl Nordell, George and Alessandra Lopez, Eddie Montalvo, Joe Campbell, Lee Paige, Donivan Darius, Don Davey, Clifton Smith, Fernando Smith, Brian Travis, David Jones, Scott Novak, Sean McInerney, Mike Dottier, Bert Pena, Al Smith, Seneca McMillan, Daryle Tally, Pat Garrett, Diane Robertelli, Tammy Wolley and my godchild Noelle Clay.

We have so many more friends that I apologize if we missed you. Please understand that we still love and care for all of you. No one got hurt making this book.

How Did I Get Here?

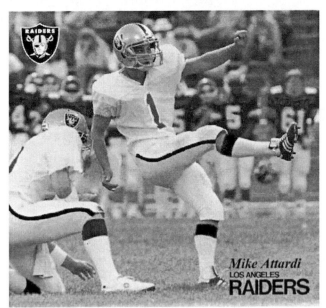

Mike Attardi
LOS ANGELES
RAIDERS

This is the only photo I have of me kicking with the Raiders.
We didn't have mobile phones with cameras back then.

I was in Thousand Oaks, California. It was one of the hottest days of the year. I was there for the Los Angeles Raiders summer camp. I had one of the greatest practices in my NFL career. I made all eight field goals during our full contact scrimmage and the guys all knew my name. We were all running back to the locker. Most of us were out of breath and sweating. I knew with my performance that day that I had made it hard for them to let me go. We all knew that the team had to cut to the 52 player roster and I was on the chopping block.

As I was sitting down in the locker room, sweat was pouring from my head. I took off my helmet and my number 4 jersey. I was holding both as if I never wanted to let them go. I noticed to the left of me was future Hall of Famer Howie Long. Even he was trying to catch his breath too. Sitting to my right was future Hall of Famer Marcus Allen. Next to him were world class sprinters and Olympic gold medal winners, Willie Gault and Ron Brown. Then I saw Hall of Famer Ronnie Lott and Roger Craig walk past me to head to the showers.

My heart was racing so fast. I didn't know if it was from running sprints or from my disbelief of where I was sitting! I was surrounded by greatness. Guys who have played the game of football at a Hall of Fame level. I sat there thinking, how did I get here? How am I in this room with so much talent? Why was I chosen to kick for the Raiders? I'm just a small town kid from Long Branch, New Jersey.

Then Hall of Fame Coach, Art Shell, walked into the room. He said, "I need four Rookies tomorrow to speak to a hundred high school football players. I need Attardi, McGlockton, Roth and Smith. I also need a veteran, so Elvis Patterson please join them. First, I want to see if you guys know what you're talking about before you talk to these kids. I'm going to ask you one simple question. What is the most important meal of the day?"

Elvis Patterson, with the whole locker room filled, stood up and shouted, "Breakfast." Coach Shell replies, "That is correct Elvis. Now tell me why breakfast is the most important meal of the day?" Elvis looked around then turned to the coach and said, "Breakfast is the most important meal of the day. He paused for a moment. Then he said, the reason is because if I'm not home before breakfast, my wife is going to kill me." All the guys in the locker room began laughing. They were falling on the floor in sheer joy after a hard day's practice.

Coach Shell replies, "You're not talking to those kids Elvis!" It had to be one of the funniest things I've ever heard anyone say on the spot. At that moment, I felt like I was part of something special. I felt like I did belong and I was there because I earned it. I was like everyone in that locker room, we all had a story about how we got there. Some had raw talent and some like me had to practice much harder.

After the laughter had stopped, I came to the realization of why I was there. Then one of the team's assistants approached me. He told me that Steve Ortmayer wanted to see me in his office. Steve was our General

Manager and special teams coach. The only thing going through my head was that Steve was about to tell me how great I did in practice today. You see, the reason I was in the Raiders camp was because of Jeff Jaeger. I was assigned to put pressure on him. Jeff was an all-pro kicker for three seasons and I knew I was climbing an uphill battle.

When I arrived in Steve's office he sat me down to tell me that the Raiders would no longer need my services. I remember feeling a crushing blow to my chest. I still remember that feeling. I knew it was difficult for Steve to tell me, since we had grown to be friends. He explained that Jaeger settled his contract. He also said that if anything should happen to Jeff during the season, they would call me back. They had to get to the 52-man roster cut and so I was released.

Steve also knew that I was not feeling well. I was kicking with a partial torn groin. When you're 22, you think you are invincible and nothing is going to happen to you. That was my outlook. The very thought of me becoming hurt was not even on my radar, especially when I was with the Raiders. The Silver and Black! Al Davis's hitmen!

Before I could get back into the locker room to gather my stuff, owner Al Davis pulled me aside. He said, "Son, the Raider organization was proud to have you here during camp. You are among the very best players in the world and you will find another opportunity soon. The Raiders wish you much success." Al looked at me dead in my eyes and walked away. He was not a man who had time for small talk. He was all about his Raiders and "Just Win Baby!" I appreciated and respected Al Davis. He was a great owner.

That day was magical and sad at the same time. As I was cleaning out my locker, Marcus Allen came up to me. He said, "You've done what most little boys only dream about bro, don't let it get you down. You'll be back!" I smiled and gave him a man-hug. He was right. I was told all my life by different people that I would never make it to the NFL and there I was with the Los Angeles Raiders having a moment with Marcus. That was not the end, it was the beginning of a new chapter in my life.

As I was clearing out my locker I had one thought going on in my head. I was not able to go out the next day and talk to those high school players. I had been cut. What would I have said to them anyway? I wasn't in the right frame of mind to give an inspirational speech to kids when I was fighting my own demons. I got into my car and drove back to Los Angeles and checked into the Westin Airport Hotel. I was frustrated and began pacing the floor. I had so many thoughts going on in my head while in a brief loneliness. How am I going to tell my dad? I don't want to disappoint him. I don't want to let him down. He was so proud of me and I felt like I failed him.

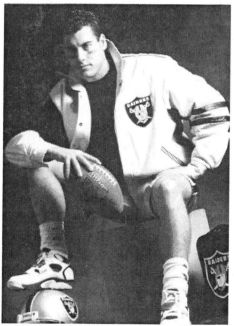
24 years old with the Los Angeles Raiders

I was proud of him too. He was a champion when he played football in high-school in the 50's. Later, he was an All American, Major League Baseball player with the Kansas City Athletics farm team. His friends called him "Iron Mike." He was also a highly-decorated Korean War hero who was humble about his service to his country. He did it all!

But, his career with the MLB was cut short when his father went blind from diabetes. My dad quit professional baseball and returned home to Long Branch to help take care of his family. He never got to finish his dreams. Now, here I was, following his footsteps of almost getting there. It was hard for me to call him right then. This is a man who used to hold over a hundred footballs every practice while I was a kid. He believed in me.

Before I went to the NFL Camp my father and family had a surprise celebration party for me. Now I had to call him and tell him that his son got released from the Los Angeles Raiders. I felt so bad.

I just sat there in my hotel room near Los Angeles Airport. I kept staring out my hotel window watching the planes landing and taking off. It was almost like my own experience up to that point. My life was taking off at one point and the sky was my limit. Then in one sweeping moment, I was being grounded. I was like that airplane that had a rough landing a few seconds ago.

My eyes were growing heavy and I knew that I was sleep deprived from the drive from Thousand Oaks to Los Angeles. The chair I was sitting on was leather and it reclined. It was so comfortable that I took some time that I needed to lick my wounds.

I picked up the hotel phone to call my father a few hours later. My mother answered the phone and I asked to speak to Dad. Without hesitation she says, "What's wrong? Did you get cut? If you did, it's their loss Michael. You have nothing to be ashamed of." I replied, "Yes, I got cut. Can you pick me up tomorrow at Newark Airport around 5pm?" My father got on the phone and said, "This too shall pass son. Let's get that leg healthy and ready for another opportunity. I'll pick you up tomorrow at the airport. Safe travels my son. Hey, I'm very proud of you. You did what other little boys only dream of doing. You made it! No one can ever take that away from you." That was exactly what Marcus Allen had told me only several hours ago. I guess great minds think alike.

Till this day, I have kids ask me what was my greatest football injury? They all guess a torn muscle, a broken leg, a sprained ankle or a broken bone. My reply, "The greatest injury ever was when I got my feelings hurt the day I was cut from the Raiders. I knew that I was not going to be in that locker- room, on that field or with my teammates anymore. I got my feelings hurt. That was my greatest injury ever in football." Now it's time to heal.

I was very fortunate to have the opportunity to play in college and in the NFL. I wasn't there for long but the journey to get there seemed like it was eternality. The many sacrifices and dedication a player has to endure is life changing. As a player, you need to put yourself in a different mindset than anyone else. The way you train, eat and practice will separate you from the others who want to achieve your same goal. My father had a saying, "If it was that easy, everyone would be doing it." Never was there a day easy and most of the guys I played football with seemed to quit and moved on with their lives. Now, it was my turn. I was tired and scared and I knew that I had to reinvent myself. Just the thought of this made me exhausted.

My Family-A Humble Beginning

I went straight to bed that night in Los Angeles and had a few dreams. I remember dreaming of my childhood and how I made this journey. My dream flashbacks started with me growing up in my hometown of Long Branch, New Jersey. There I was with my grandfather, Daniel, sitting on our house porch in rocking chairs. I loved listening to my grandfather tell his stories about our home and his colorful past. Daniel was like a character out of a Broadway show. I never got tired of hearing about his wild adventures and many achievements. In fact, his stories had inspired me and helped me understand how to be persistent and stay focused.

My grandfather Daniel gave me a picture, which years later had much more meaning then it did when he gave it to me. In the photo, he was dressed up like the famous actor Charlie Chaplin. Daniel Gesualdi was my mother's father. He and was born in Foggia, Italy. Later, he was a carpenter in New Jersey. Then he took a long unknowing trip out to Hollywood in the 1920's. He had discovered that Hollywood was hiring carpenters to build movie sets. They were making double the wage of the local builders in New Jersey at the time.

He arrived in Hollywood and the studios hired him. While he was working on a movie set, an accident happened to an actor. They needed someone to fill the actor's part. My grandfather had the right look and skills. He was immediately hired as a stunt double for Charlie Chaplin. He appeared in several silent films in the 1920's. Some of the films included: The Kid in 1923; Women of Paris in 1925; Gold Rush in 1928 and The Circus. My grandfather missed his family in New Jersey so much and left Hollywood for good.

In 1930, he moved back to Newark, New Jersey. He worked on a construction crew that was building the tallest skyscraper in the world. It was the Empire State Building. He quit that job six months later, after one of his friends was blown off the building and died. My grandfather once said, "I made it only to the 38th floor. That was the craziest job in

7

My Grandfather, Daniel Gesualdi, was Charlie Chaplin's stunt double and in drag as an actor. Back in those days, females were not allowed to do stunts.

the world. The winds were so strong up there, even the heavy iron beams were moving like feathers." He worked for the union for several years as a mason in New Jersey.

Then during the early 1940's he served in World War II. He was a construction foreman. He oversaw building the living quarters at Fort Hancock in Sandy Hook, New Jersey. In 1947, at the end of World War II, my grandfather bought a house. He moved his family from Newark to the city of Long Branch on the New Jersey Shore.

The 1905 house was no ordinary house. It was owned by a famous MET opera singer by the name of Amelia Galicurcci. She was an Italian opera singer who sang for the kings and queens in Europe. If you didn't know the story about our house, my grandfather would make sure that he would tell you. He loved that house. He took better care of it then his own health.

I grew up in a large three story, six thousand square foot, Victorian House. It was on a huge property near Monmouth University in Long Branch, New Jersey. The house was big but our family lived humbly. My sisters, Michelle and Francine and I used to call our house the "Westwood

Manor." Everything looks huge when you're young. The house was made from brick and wood. My grandfather added electricity and heating to the house in 1948.

My mother Frances and father Michael during their
Honeymoon in Florida 1959

My mother and father meet in 1957 when my father was just released from active duty in the Army. He spent several years on active reserve as a military policeman and also worked for the Pennsylvania railroad as a security guard.

We had the most exciting life. My mother and father provided a very loving home with Italian traditions and customs. My sisters and I did a lot together too. We went to the beach and to Great Adventure Theme Park. We rode our bikes all the time and had picnics in the park. We had watermelon fights and acorn battles. We also liked to catch fireflies every hot summer night. It was like a scene from a Norman Rockwell painting. My sisters even made me play with their Barbie dolls. I had to always be Ken or I was out of the play date. We were living on the Jersey Shore and life growing up in the 1970's. It was fun and adventurous. Our shirt collars were wide and we all had wild hair like Little Orphan Annie.

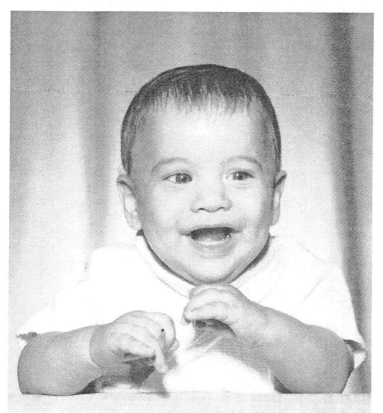

I was born Michael D. Attardi on March 15, 1967, in Long Branch, New Jersey.

Growing Up in Westwood Manor

Our House "Westwood Manor" in Long Branch, New Jersey. My sisters and I invented that name for our house. When you're young everything looks big!

At one point, my sisters and I shared the entire second floor of the house. Our parents may have wanted some space from us. I would! We were free spirited children always looking for a good time and new adventures. We learned not to be afraid of the dark as we walked together down long, dark hallways to reach a bathroom.

During the 1950's, our relatives from Newark would come down to the Jersey Shore to visit the "Westwood Manor." The house soon became the favorite family meeting place. They used to play cards, roll dice and play bingo. That's what close Italian families did back in the day. As you know, there were no iPhones to distract them. Everyone just spoke loud like they were yelling. That's how Italians speak to one another. Loudly and with quick hand gestures.

But, my grandparents became tired of family members showing up unannounced. They always came with big appetites and were very thirsty for wine. Millie became a short order cook to everyone. My grandfather said the house was becoming a free-for-all. It all stopped in 1972! I was 5 years old when my grandparents converted the second and third floors into separate apartments. And, they began to rent them to tenants. That move made a lot of our "Niki-Newark" families upset. No more summer party house on the Jersey Shore. My core family was sad, since we all loved to have our "Niki-Newark" extended family around us. They were so much fun! I remember crying when I heard that the parties were going to end.

My immediate family lived in the apartment on the third floor of our house. My grandparents, Daniel and Mildred, lived on the first floor of "Westwood Manor." My Aunt Donna, my mother's sister, also lived on the first floor in her own room that my grandfather built for her. Aunt Donna had this 1970's blue shaggy rug that you were not able to see your feet once you stepped on it. That was "groovy" back then and we loved visiting her to step on that rug and listen to the Beatles on 45's.

Michelle, Francine and I grew up with my mother's parents. My sisters and I had our own rooms on the third floor. I'd sleep there every night except for Friday. On Friday nights, I'd sneak out of my bedroom. I'd venture down those long, winding wooden creaking steps. My journey ended when I reached my grandparent's apartment. Then I'd crawl onto the couch where my grandmother "Millie" used to sleep. She was always watching T.V. Don't ask me why, but she chose to sleep on the couch

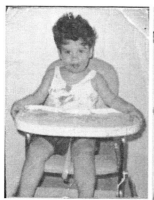

Life was one big party at "Westwood Manor"

rather then to sleep with my grandfather. I think it was because he snored.

When I was five years old I had to have surgery to get my tonsils out. This was the day that would change my life forever. The surgery caused a speech impediment and I was never the same. I was told that I had been speaking fluently before the surgery. I have flashbacks about that day but I can't put the puzzle together. All I knew was that I was not able to put two words together anymore. I was frustrated and my family knew it.

My mother, my sister Michelle and me.

One night when I was around seven years old, I snuck down stairs to sleep with my grandmother. We watched Johnny Carson and laughed together until my eyes would close shut. She used to let me watch Johnny Carson on late night television. Johnny was the Jimmy Fallon of yesteryear. How cool was that?

A few nights later, Johnny Carson had the singer Mel Tillis on his show. I was never a huge fan of country music, but I saw something special in his singing. Mel had a beautiful clear voice that was nice to listen to. After Mel Tillis' song, Johnny began to interview him. I was surprised to hear Mel Tillis speak. He was stuttering on national television.

My grandmother and I had listened to this incredible singer. Then during his interview, he had a problem putting two words together. I was shocked and happy at the same time. I said to my grandmother, "If Mel

Tellis can sing, I can sing. My grandmother said, "You can do anything you want if you put your heart into it."

Whereas, my grandfather, Daniel, was so mad that I had a speech impediment that he used to scare me not to stutter. One day I was helping him make a nightstand table and he asked me how I was doing in school. I started to tell him a story but I was stuttering so bad that he stopped me. He grabbed me by my shoulders and said, "You speak normal or I will smack you in your mouth!" When I got older, I understood that his generation did not know how to handle people who were different. He was scared that people would make fun of me and think I was stupid. Deep inside, I knew he cared for me. He only wanted the best for me.

My grandfather was not a patient man because he was from the school of hard knocks. He was a fighter. I grew closer to him when I got older. In fact, I'll never forget the time he finally said, "I love you." It was on his death bed. He had just finished telling me a story about Charlie Chaplin. It was a story I must have heard a hundred times but I acted like it was the first time I had heard it. He pulled me closer to him and with a soft voice he said, "I never had a son. You're the son I never had. I am so proud of you. You have come a long way and that is how champions are made."

That generation of men did not know how to show affection. They grew up in a hard, tough world and they wanted us to be as tough. Saying "I love you" was for a mother to say, not a grandfather. Times have changed. That was the last conversation I had with my grandfather. He passed away that night in peace.

My Grandma Mildred, would always pray for me. She'd go to church every day. That is not an exaggeration. She went to St. Michael's Roman Catholic Church EVERYDAY! She used to take me on Saturday and Sunday and make me say the rosary with her. Millie taught me all the prayers and I learned about all the saints and holy days of obligation. Who needed Sunday school when I had Millie?

Millie would drive us to church, 30 minutes before Mass started. There were very few people in church sitting in the pews before Mass. She always wanted to get the best seat in the house and several older women would challenge her for the space. I never knew how territorial sweet little old church ladies can get when it comes to their position in church. It was so quiet in church that I could hear Millie pray for me. It killed her that I had a speech impediment.

She was on a mission from God to help cure me, even if it took going to church every day, as she did. I heard her one day talking to another church lady who suggested that the devil had my tongue. Millie took her purse and wacked the lady in the head and said, "The Devil must have taken over my bag as well!" The lady in disbelief walked away in a swift manner. We never saw that lady in church again.

Every Saturday and Sunday, we'd wake up to the aromas of Grandma Millie's coffee, eggs and ham. She would also be making her tomato gravy. That's correct, the Sicilians called their tomato sauce "gravy." She would let it simmer on low while we went to church.

After church, we'd go to Valentino's Butcher Shop that had fresh wood saw dust on the floor. I didn't understand why wood dust was always on the floor. Then one day when the butcher cut a cow's leg he must have hit its artery. Blood from the cow squirted onto my shirt and all over the floor. I now knew why the saw dust was there. It was there to soak up the blood. Then, as every Sunday, we continued to watch the butcher make fresh sausage for our Sunday's dinner.

When we left the butcher shop we'd walk across the street to Baldanza's Italian Bakery. We'd get freshly made Italian breads and pastries. I didn't mind going to church since I knew the result would be a chocolate éclair, crumb buns or a sugar donut. Baldanza's was a kids' dream come true. I felt like I was in the movie Willie Wonka and the Chocolate factory. The glass displays in the bakery were like works of art. Each display flowed with different colors and edible treats. I used to say to my grandmother, "If you look at them any longer, you're sure to gain 5 more pounds." She would always give me a courtesy laugh having to hear that every Sunday.

When we returned from home, My sisters and I would hide under Millie's kitchen table. We were like little rats waiting until she left the kitchen. We would sneak out of my hiding place and steal a piece of the fresh Italian bread and dip it into the tomato gravy. Millie's gravy was the greatest gravy of all time. She could have won major awards for that gravy. If only we knew how to bottle it and sell it, Millie could have been a millionaire for all we knew.

For years, Millie would accuse my grandfather of this heinous act of the mysterious dip. Then one day, I was finally caught with gravy all over my face under her kitchen table. Millie said, "Are you eating my gravy when it's not done? If you do that you will get worms." The thought of getting worms was not a pretty picture. I saw what worms can do to dogs at our last veterinarian visit with our dog Bonnie. That was the last time I performed the sneak the gravy trick. It was only years later that I realized that she was kidding. How can you get worms from eating tomatoes that are raw? Duh! Maybe that's why I was called "Mr. Gullible!"

My sister, Michelle and me at three and six years old

My grandmother spoiled me. She protected me. She was my second mother and never did she allow me to get down on myself or quit. Millie would say, "Quitters are average, and you're not average. You're like Superman and someday you'll get rid of that Kryptonite of a speech problem."

One of the funniest stories I can tell you about my grandmother, Millie, is the shoe tapping story. We watched the movie Singing in the Rain with Gene Kelly. When I saw Gene dance, I wanted to be a tap dancer. My grandfather was not too fond of little boys who wanted to be dancers. He was grooming me to be a football player, not a dancer. The thought of this bothered him. My grandmother was different, she didn't care what I did as long as I tried to do my best.

I bugged my mother and father to get me tap shoes for weeks. Then one day, Millie came home with these shinny leather shoes. Millie took several Coca-Cola tin bottle caps and tacked them into their soles. She handed me the shoes and told me to start tapping. I started to tap and I was horrible. But that did not stop Millie from clapping and singing the song Singing in the Rain.

I thought I was Gene Kelly until I started sliding across her wood kitchen floors as if I were on a piece of sheeted ice. I felt stupid and clumsy. I fell a few times but kept on trying to dance. My thought was, if Gene Kelly can do it, I could do it too.

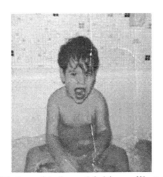

At three years old, I used to love drinking milk, take a bath and
get into a warm robe 50 years later I'm still doing it.

Millie was laughing so hard that she ran to the bathroom because she peed in her pants. That was the last time I tried to tap dance with coke bottle caps. I tapped danced years later in the show No No Nanette and she took credit for teaching me how to tap dance. Who could argue? Millie would always let you fail first before she would save you. I remember her saying, "A good failure will make anyone wiser and stronger!"

Every Sunday was family day in our house. Our dinners were like a Ernie Barnes painting. There was always more food on the table that could ever be eaten during one sitting. We ate like it was our last supper. We would have a table filled with over 14 people eating, laughing and telling wild stories of our week. These were the days of no mobile phones or iPads. We communicated with real conversation and stories. Face to face using eye contact and talking with our hands. That's how Italian's talk, with our hands. Not to forget the volume level of our speaking voices raised up several notches.

My first birthday 1968, Michelle, my father, My Grandmother, Me and Grandfather Daniel

My 10th Birthday with family

You see, Italian's love to speak over one another. They believe that what they are saying at that moment is the most important thing in the world. As if it was going to stop world hunger or cure cancer. At one point, my grandfather would stand up and shout, "Shut up your face." My sisters and I would crack up every time he said that. All the kids in school would say that Italian's used that phrase all the time and we would deny it. Than a song came out in 1981 by Joe Dolce called *Shaddap you face*. We would sing that song all the time and he would laugh.

There were difficulties at times too. We hated hearing my grandfather verbally abuse my father. My grandfather wanted my father to be more than he was. My father was the hardest working man I knew. When I look back now it amazes me to think that my father could have crushed my grandfather with one hand.

My father was a gentle giant with huge arms of steel. He had arms like a super hero. All those years working for his father as a brick layer made my dad a strong man. My father was respectful and kind and would never retaliate out of respect for my mother.

We liked playing in our large yard. We played freeze tag, hide and go seek and dodge ball. In fact, all the neighborhood kids liked it too. They would come over to our house for pick-up games of football and baseball. We even lined the side yard like a football field with white paint. My grandfather was upset at us that he made us go out and buy green paint and repaint the yard. My grandfather was always trying to make a point.

We had a little vineyard in the backyard where my grandfather and I used to pick the grapes and make wine. He used to take the dead fish heads and bury them near the roots of the grape vines. One day I asked, "Why do you bury fish heads near the grapes." He replied, "What's it to you? Are you keeping track of my fish heads? Have you ever smelt a fish head several days in a hot garbage can? Who in the hell wants to smell that?" I was curious and wanted to know why. That's what a normal eight year old would do. Ask questions.

My grandmother had more patience and told me that the fish heads will make the soil more fertile for growing. She called it compound. The time that it took him to chew me a new butt and not answer the question was just like my grandfather. He had no patience. He would say, "Kids should be seen and never heard." Then he wonders why I had a speech impediment and I hid from him?

We used to pick those grapes and put them in a large wooden tub. My shirts would end up purple. Back then there was no liquid cleaner like Shout! The only Shout I had, was my mother shouting how stupid I was to wear a white shirt to pick grapes. It wasn't so bad because my grandfather would let me walk on the grapes in my bare feet to crush them. For some reason, I thought that was the coolest thing in the world. It was also the weirdest feeling when those grapes are squirting through your toes.

Even though I was only eight years old, my grandfather used to let me sample a taste of wine. He used to call it the "Nectar of Life. Our wine was a huge hit at family parties. He would always take full credit for his winemaking skills and called me his mule. That was exactly what I was to him but I still loved and respected him. He taught me many great lessons. He even taught me how to fix broken things through reverse engineering.

Life was great at "Westwood Manor." It was paradise to us!

Don't Mess with My Mother

My mother was a tough Italian-American woman. She protected her children and taught us right from wrong. One day, I came home crying from school. My mother asked me what had gone wrong, as she wiped away my tears. I told her that I was pulled out of the line by the principal today during lunch. She asked if I did something wrong. I told her the truth. I learned at a young age to never lie to my mother. If I did, she would know.

Me at 8 years old

Two boys were making fun of my stutter and they both punched me in the chest. My heart was racing. I couldn't control my anger so I punched them back in the nose. I knocked one of them to the ground. I had blood on my fist. Then, a large hand grabbed me by my neck and pulled me with excessive force out of the lunch line. It was the principal and he only saw me punch the kids back. He held me by my collar, almost choking me, and took me into his office. He told me that I was going to be expelled and he was calling my mother later that day.

When I got home, I had never seen my mother so mad in my life. She put my sister Francine and I in the car and raced to the school. My mother must have gone through every stop sign. My mom arrived in record time at the school and stormed into the principal's office. His secretary told her that she would announce her. My mother gave her the hand to the face and kicked open the principle's door like Arnold Schwarzenegger in the movie Terminator.

My mother then stormed into the principal's office. She grabbed him by his shirt collar, and said, "If you ever put your hands on my son again, you will regret the day you were born! If my husband finds out that you attacked our son, it will be your last day on earth! Do you understand me?" The principal did not know what to say. In fact, I thought in that moment I may not be the only one that had a stuttering problem. He was not able to get two words out in fear that my mom was going to kick his butt.

She let go of his collar and stormed out his office. Once again, she gave her hand to the face of the secretary. When we got back in the car my mother started to hyper ventilate and then broke down crying. She was one of the toughest women I ever met and everyone knew not to mess with her. Deep inside, she was sweet and kind. But, you couldn't mess with any of her children. Especially when it came to me. I was her only son.

That's when I realized that when my mom told you to do something, you'd better do it! No questions asked, no time goes by, and never would I say no to her. The principal apologized to me the next day. The other two boys were expelled after he'd heard the full story. Later, those two boys ended up becoming my good friends because I stood up to them. I've been in a lot of fights over my speech impediment in the past. But, I'll never forget this one. It was the only time that my mother had to come to school to rescue me from an adult. After that day, the principal never failed to say hello to me. He also made sure that I was being taken care of the rest of my time at Elberon Elementary School.

My mother was always about 'right and wrong' and she never let us get away with anything. She taught us how to "Man up!" If we did wrong, we had to address adversity and issues that we had created with true humility. I have countless stories of her teaching us about how to live a clean and honest life. I cherish her teachings and have passed them onto my sons. That is what life is all about, teaching and guiding our children to do the right things.

Original Mickey Mouse drawn by Marc Davis

My mother always knew that I loved art. She encouraged me to draw and paint during my playtime. I was a huge Disney fan and she used to read me all the Disney classics with the animation drawings. So, when I was eight years old, my mother took me and my sister Francine to the Monmouth Mall to meet some Disney artists. We were young kids, we had no idea of who they were. We only knew they were a few old guys who created Snow White and the Seven Dwarfs and Pinocchio. They were Frank Thomas, Ollie Johnston, Ward Kimble and Marc Davis. They were four of Walt Disney's Nine Old Men, the greatest animation artists of all-time.

These artists were showing the crowd how to draw and make animation come to life. Marc Davis looked around the crowd and asked for a volunteer. My sister Francine raised my arm up and Marc chose us. He had my sister and I assist him during his presentation of how to draw Mickey Mouse. When he picked me out of the crowd, it was like time had stopped and everything around me was in slow motion.

When he asked me for my name, I stammered and said Miiichael At ttt tardi. The crowd laughed. Immediately, Marc said, "Okay, Michael Attardi, who is your favorite Disney character?" I said, "MMMMMickey MMMMouse." Once again, the crowd laughed louder. Don't forget, this was in the 70's and no one knew about being politically correct.

Marc came in quickly and said, "Mickey Mouse. You know, he's my favorite too." I smiled. Marc picked up his pastel and started to draw Mickey with circles. Marc completed it in seconds. It was the most amazing display of art I had ever seen up to that moment.

Marc tore the Mickey artwork off his drawing pad and gave it to me. That drawing has been one of my most prized possessions. That piece of art inspired me to want to become an animator and a director of film. That simple act of kindness with Marc had instilled the confidence I needed. It was also an "a-ha" moment. My mother on the way home stopped a local art store and bought us some art supplies. Francine and I went home and started to draw. I gravitated more towards drawing houses and landscapes. At one point of my life, I thought I wanted to be an architect. I would draw designs for houses and was highly inspired by Frank Lloyd Wright.

Elberon School, Learning Life's Lessons

With my lifelong friend, Vinny Fiore

I lived about two miles away from my elementary school, which was Elberon Elementary. We played kickball every single day. Kickball was a way of life for us. It was also the sport that made me popular. It meant so much to me that I would wake up early and walk to my friend's house's at 6:00 am to gather up the gang. My first stop was at Matt Baker's house, then Vinny Fiore's, Peter Newman's, Jody Creed's, Joey DiBiase's and Brian Guzzman's houses. At every house we stopped by, each one of the mothers would have some sort of breakfast treat waiting for us. By the time we got to school, most of us were stuffed.

We used to have some fierce games of kickball. Vinny Fiore and I were the big kickers and our classmates would not allow us to be on the same team. They called me Sasquatch, better known as Bigfoot and Vinny was called Thunder foot. We used to kick the ball over the school's roof and everyone would get mad at us for holding up the game.

We must have climbed up the side of the school to that roof several times a day to get the ball. Then we all got smart and moved to the back of the school at the baseball diamond. There was no fence, just a lot of open land. When Vinny Fiore would come up to kick, I would move all the way back in the outfield. The ball would fly so high in the sky that I would have to track it down with radar to make the catch. I still believe that is what made me a great outfielder in baseball. Vinny would return the favor many times when I came up to kick. Always robbing me of a homerun. The team that won was based on Vinny or myself making the last big kick before the bell rang for school.

If we finished the game before the school bell rang, we all would go to the Elberon general store to buy candy. The store had these little paper brown bags that we would place about 40 to 50 pieces of candy in for only a dollar. We used to buy jaw breakers, gobstopper's, red hots and gum. When we had left-over money, we would chip in and buy baseball and football cards so we could flip them.

Matt Baker was one of my best friends growing up during my adolescence. We did everything together. We played baseball, kick ball, hockey, football and anything with a ball. We had so much fun creating off-the-wall word scenarios with Mad Libs. I had my very first sleepover at Matt's house and he had two brothers.

Matt and I were so close that if anyone would make fun of me because of my stuttering, he would go after them like he was my protector. He also never allowed anyone to talk behind my back. Matt would shut it down the moment anyone would say anything about me. I had a lot of respect for Matt. He was the older brother I never had.

One-day Matt Baker and I were walking over the railroad tracks past the Elberon train station, when we saw some people buying newspapers from the machine. I had a great idea. We put in 25 cents and we'd take out all the papers. Once we did that, we walked around to all the businessmen and sold them for 50 cents each. We had a pretty good business going on until a few weeks later we got caught by the paper distribution guy. We had to payback every cent!

A few days later, Matt and I dressed up like Cub Scouts and collected over $45 dollars in donations in front of Foodtown in the West End. We were doing just fine until the head Cub Scout leader of our local den caught us and we had to give the money we collected to their Pack. Who knew? We really didn't know if what we were doing was such a big deal at the age of 10. We were just trying to make a buck!

My lifelong friend Matt Baker and me playing hockey

That did not stop us from inventing new and creative ways of making money. My grandmother Millie, used to collect Christmas cards and had accumulated what seemed like over a thousand of them. She kept them in her closet. The church would send them to her in the mail and she would donate money for the cards. I had asked her what she was going to do with the cards and she told me I could take them.

I called my other best friend, Eric Peduto. Matt, Eric and I separated the cards into ten cards per pack. We canvased our neighborhood and sold one pack for a dollar each. We sold over 100 packs and made exactly one hundred dollars. A small fortune for any 10-year-old. After two days of selling, my mother received several phone calls from neighbors with complaints. The cards we were selling were not only old, but many were used! We had no idea. Why would my grandmother save used Christmas cards? We had to go around to every house and give back all the money.

A week later, Matt and I were at the Elberon candy store buying baseball cards. When we left, we walked past a medal grate. There is something about medal grates that boys just love. I looked inside the grate and saw a medium sized, blue bag. I called Matt over and we found two sticks. Together with the precision of two surgeon's, we carefully raised the bag through the grate and pulled it through. We opened the bag and there was money inside of it. I'm not talking dollar bills, I'm talking one-hundred-dollar bills. We closed the bag and ran! Never did we look back, we just ran as fast as we could.

When we got to Matt's house, we sprinted upstairs to his room and put the bag on his bed. We had to be careful because we did not want his brothers to find out. There we were just staring at the money all laid out. We have never seen that much money before in our life. We counted seventeen hundred dollars. I said, "What the hell are we going to do with all this money?" Matt replied, "I think we can buy a house with that!" We were 10 years old, maybe you could buy a house, who knew? Matt said, "Someone lost this money and we have to get it back to them."

I agreed. We walked to my house and showed the bag and all the money to my father. He was totally stunned as he said, "Where in the hell did you boys get this money?" We told him the whole story. Immediately, he drove us to the Long Branch Police Station and gave the money to an officer. Inside the bag was a bank slip that we did not see and it had the name of the owner. The police called the man and he came to retrieve his money. The man was a local doctor who had an office in Deal, New Jersey. When he got off the train from New York, he must have dropped the bag and it fell down the grate. The doctor assumed that someone on the train stole the bag and he had reported it to the New Jersey Transit Police. When the doctor arrived, he thanked both Matt and me and gave us a two hundred dollars finder's fee as a thank you for our honesty. Matt and I were not expecting that. We learned that by doing the right thing that day really does payoff.

Then, when I was in sixth grade, I found out that Matt got into some bad trouble and was sent away. Although I haven't seen him since that time, we recently reconnected and were able to share all the stories of the time that we had missed together. I still consider him to be one of my close friends. You don't have to physically touch someone or see that person to know that they are still your lifelong friend.

I had another bright idea that I thought was fool proof. With Halloween only a few days away, I convinced my friend, Eric to come out with me to trick-or-treat two days before Halloween. We thought by going two days early, we would get all the good candy first. We got into our costumes and took a few pillow cases for all the potential loot we would collect. The plan sounded like a good idea at the time.

When we arrived at our first house, our neighbor answered the door. He seemed to have no idea that it wasn't Halloween and he was scrambling around the house looking for candy. He kept repeating, "I have no clue where my wife hid the candy." When he couldn't find any candy, he took out his wallet and gave us both a dollar.

After that, things started turning badly for us. Every house we went to, the residents would give us a piece of fruit because they didn't buy any candy yet. To top it off, we got lost. If it wasn't for a mother who knew who we were from school, Eric and I would have still been walking around Elberon. She let us use her phone. We were picked up by Eric's Mom who was not happy. She told Eric he was grounded. Neither one of us were allowed to leave our yards after that. My mom wasn't mad because I brought home a pillowcase of fruit and she made two apple pies with them. When life gives you apples, make apple pie!

Then there was the time that I asked Eric to go out Christmas Caroling with me to raise money for us to buy Christmas gifts for our families. Eric was all for the adventure. Later that night when we went out to sing, we were only getting a dollar from the first few houses. Then we went to this one house and the lady recognized me from St. Michael's Church. I used to sing in the church choir and she asked if we were raising money for the church. Before I could say anything, she handed us a $20 bill. Eric and I just looked at each other in disbelief and thanked her and moved on. When we walked away we gave each other a huge high-five! When we went to the next house, we said that we were raising money for St. Michael's Church. We sang a few songs and once again, we received another $20.

This went on for the rest of the night and we had about $450 bulging out of our pockets. It was so cold that night and we were both getting tired, but Eric wanted to press on to see if we can get to $500. The last house we got to, we knocked at the door. Never in my wildest thoughts did I think that the person that was going to answer that door was none other than Monsignor Bradley of St. Michael's Church.

Before I could say anything to Eric, he said, "Hi, we're raising money for St. Michael's Church by singing." Monsignor Bradley asked, "How much money have you boys raised?" Eric's response, "$450 dollars." Before I could say another word, Monsignor Bradley said, "Well thank you very much boys. That was very thoughtful of you. Especially this time of year when our Lord's birthday is coming up soon." I was a deer in headlights!

If my grandmother ever found out what I had done, she would've disowned me. Without skipping a beat, I played along and handed him all our money. I turned to Eric and said, "This is Monsignor Bradley of St. Michael's Church. As you can see he's very happy that we brought the money straight to him." Eric just looked at me with a blank stare. We gave all the money to the Monsignor. On the long walk home Eric turned to me and said, "What are the chances that the last house we went to was Monsignor Bradley's of Saint Michael's church?" I turned to him without hesitation and said, "Let's just call it divine intervention."

That Sunday, our family sat in the front pew of the church. Monsignor was looking at me the whole time or maybe I was just being paranoid. At the end of mass, he made the church announcements. He asked me to stand up in front of all the 400 plus parishioners. The only thought that was playing in my head was that I had a one-way ticket to hell and Monsignor was about to hand it to me on a silver platter. Monsignor asked me to sing a Christmas song. I took a deep breath and looked over to my grandmother who lit up like a Christmas tree as I started to sing "Silent Night" in front of the whole church.

My father had a dumbfounded look on his face as if he knew that I was up to no good. My mother just ran with it knowing that singing was the only way that I could communicate fluently without stuttering. My sister Michelle was just laughing because she knew I got caught doing something bad and I was gonna get away with it anyway. It was almost like the time that she caught me and our neighbor Richie trying to smoke a cigarette under our house porch. She ran to my mother and told her but my mother didn't say anything to me about it. Then my father came home and he shoved a pack of cigarettes in my mouth and told me to smoke them. That was a lesson well learned.

As I was singing I had all these thoughts racing through my mind, I realized that if Millie was happy then no one was going to touch me. I was known as "Teflon Mike" when it came to Millie. No matter what bad thing I did, Millie had my back and it was only seconds ago that Monsignor sang my praises. I knew, this put me at a much higher level with Millie. She saw that I had a stamp of approval from the man who was closer to God than anyone else in our community. I decided to sing better and put on a show. I sang Silent Night as if I were Whitney Houston singing the National Anthem during the 1990 Super Bowl. The only thing I didn't have was a Mach 2 G-force F-16 flyby. As I hit the last note, all 400 plus parishioners went into a cheering mode and I knew I was out of the dark forest. I was confident that God was on my side because he had taught me a lesson.

Monsignor then tells the cheering crowd that Eric and I raised $500 for the church with our beautiful voices and that one day we both will be famous singers. Monsignor Bradley was a rock star to our community. I will never forget what he did for us. He could have easily sold us down the river and made us do penance for years. Instead, he raised us for our faults without saying a word about it. His act of kindness made me a better man and a better Christian to mankind. I have never been deceitful again. And, I have no plans to start now. A lesson well learned. I cried myself to sleep that night because I felt so guilty and I knew that God was watching me. Being raised Catholic, we live with guilt as part of everyday life. If you don't feel guilt then you're not a true Catholic. I say that in a positive way. Guilt is what makes us perform righteous acts. I know Monsignor is with God and is probably having a good laugh right now.

My lifelong friend Eric Peduto with his wife Stephanie, me and my wife Colleen at Disney

We used to read the Hardy Boys Mysteries in paper back at Elberon Elementary School. My mom used to call us the Attardi boys. We always had different mysteries and adventures that my friends and I used to get into as kids. There was an old carriage house only a few doors down from us and it really looked scary. Eric and I would make up stories about the old building to scare the other neighborhood kids. Especially when you're around eight years old, your imagination starts to run wild. The lady that lived there was very quiet and we thought that her large three-story house was haunted. When you're young, all large houses are haunted.

One Saturday morning after watching the Super Friends cartoons on TV, we all gathered over Eric's house to play Evil Knievel on our bikes. Eric's neighbors were the Todd's and they had a hill that we used to play on. We used to ride our bikes up to the top and then all the way back down for hours. It seemed like it was a hundred feet high, but it was probably only about 20. After doing that for about an hour, we all got a little bored and decided to take a ride down the S-curve street in the back of our house. Earlier that week we had just gotten done reading a Hardy Boys novel that was about the boys exploring a haunted house.

We came upon the old carriage house that's about 200 yards away from the huge main house that we thought was haunted. Eric and I convinced the other kids to explore. We all finally went inside that old carriage house garage that we all were afraid of. With stealth reflexes and determination, we climbed under the fence and opened the window in the carriage house. We looked at each other like we really were one of those Hardy Boys on an adventure. We all climbed through the window and found ourselves inside a dark and cold room. A black 1950's Chevrolet was sitting there just aging away. Old farm equipment like a sickle, pitchfork and other weird tools were hanging on the wall. It looked like a movie prop set from the film Friday the 13th. To be honest, as we approached the large boxes, we were more like the Scooby Doo Gang than the Hardy Boys.

The curiosity was killing us for what was inside the large wooden travel chest. It was the same kind that travelers used to take on long steam boat voyages and adventures back in the day. In our minds, we were just about to discover the Holy Grail. I looked at Eric and dared him to open the chest. He double dared me, so I had to do it. There's something about a double dare that you just can't go back on and as kids we honored that. With the precision of a highly skilled surgeon, I opened the box. Our eyes all grew wide and we were shocked to see what was in that box. What we had thought all along was true.

The lady that owned the house was hiding a dark secret and we just discovered it. Eric said, "You were right Mike, that lady killed someone and put them in this box." The box was filled with what we had thought to be human bones. We all looked at each other and decided to run. Like little rats, we fit through that window and got under that fence faster than any Olympic gold medalist.

We went back and told my mother and father. They called the police. When the police came, it was almost like a murder scene. "Do Not Cross" tape was all around the old spooky carriage house. All five of us were next to one of three police cars as if we were still part of the investigation. The old lady was being escorted by two police officers to the carriage house. All that was going on in my mind was that our band of mystery hunters had just caught a killer. The only problem was, she didn't really look like a killer. She looked like a nice old lonely woman who was being inconvenienced on a hot summer's day. After several minutes waiting for them to emerge from the carriage house, the police and the old lady walked out. One of the officer's signaled for us to come over. Excited to hear what was going on, we all ran over to the police officer. The officer said, "So, which one of you found the dead body?" As proud investigators, we all raised our hands. The officer asked us to follow him into the carriage house with the older lady.

We all surrounded the wooden box that held what we thought were human bones. The officer turned to us and then opened the box as he said, "Good work boys, you discovered bones of a dog. Your neighbor here is a veterinarian and all these boxes are filled with animal bones. The real question is, what were all you boys doing in this carriage house in the first place?" The three other neighborhood kids just pointed at Eric and me and said, "It was their idea! They wanted to be the Hardy Boys." The lady laughed.

Eric and I took the blame and we had to cut her lawn for a whole month as a punishment. Not that bad if you consider that we were breaking and entering on her property. I see the story as a glass half full, because if you think about it, Eric and I really were the Hardy Boys. In fact, the hit show on Netflix called *Strangers Things* was based on our life growing up in Long Branch, New Jersey. Weird things happened to us all the time and we treated them as a normal way of life growing up in the 1970's.

Luck of the Italians

My Father and Sister Francine a few days before I got my bike

When I was 11 years old, I wanted a bike so badly that I hustled for jobs in my neighborhood to make money to buy one. One day I was working for this lady who owned a pharmacy in Deal, New Jersey. Her house was down the street from my great friend Randy Rosen. Randy used to tease me about having to work. His father was a successful local dentist. I remember walking over to Randy's house after a hard day's work and his mother would make us greatest lunches. The Rosen's had the coolest playroom ever in their attic. They had a pinball machine, board games and a pool table. Back then, no one had a pinball machine in their home. I would call my mom a few hours later and she would pick me up from their house. Randy and I have been friends since kindergarten. He's one of those friends that you don't have to see all the time to know that he will always have your back.

One day I was doing yard work for the lady and she made it a point to be nasty to me right from the start. I disliked working for this mean woman who always yelled at me in her raspy, demanding voice. She always treated me like I was beneath her because my father serviced her cars at the dealership. In her eyes, he was a blue collar worker. Then again, he was.

I stuck it out because I never quit anything in my life and this crummy job was not going to be the first. That day was also one of the hottest days ever on the Jersey Shore. At the young age of 10, I really thought my life was coming to an end. If I asked her for a glass of water, she would take fifty cents out of my pay. She began to pull away in her new Mercedes-Benz that her husband just bought for her and said to me, "Nothing is free in this world!" There I was, completely overheated with a dry mouth. One time when I was working for her I dunked my head in her bird bath fountain just to get cooled off. I also snuck a drink from her dirty hot garden hose. I only did that once because it was so nasty. I was sure I'd contracted some sort of disease from that!

As I sat in the shade while sweat was dripping off my forehead, my father drove into her driveway. It was like I was being freed from my jail sentence. I remember hearing the song "Help" from the Beatles in my head. My dad told that old witch that he was picking me up early. I was never so happy to leave hell at that moment. The worst chore at my house would beat the best job at the old witch's house on any given day.

When I got into his air-conditioned car, I knew at the age of 10, that manual labor was not for me and that college was on my radar. Then my father asked, "Want to go to the racetrack with Dad?" I said, "Hell yes! Is that a trick question?" He laughed. My father loved seeing me earn a tough dollar. He knew I was miserable working there. I never told him because I wanted to show him I could do it. My father was tough and I wanted to be just like him.

My father enjoyed horse racing. He had friends who were horse trainers and jockeys. He knew how to bet the ponies. If he started with $100 and all the races were over and he still had $50 or more in his pocket then that was a winning day for him. But my dad was not having much success betting on the horses that hot summer day at Monmouth Park Racetrack. In fact, he lost every race and we only had one more to go. My father turned to me and said: "Pick any two horses. Any two numbers that pop into your head." I looked at the program and saw exactly two numbers that popped out.

This was funny because I already knew what he was about to ask me from that look of desperation on his face. The look of "Oh crap! My wife is going to kill me if I don't have money for this weekend." Without hesitation, I said nine and ten.

He looked up at the odds board and says, "9 and 10? Are you kidding me? They're both 60 to one longshots. Never mind." My dad turned away in confusion and then turned back to me holding his last two dollars in his hand. He said: "This is my last two dollars. I can buy you an ice cream cone and call it a day or we can play the 9 and 10 exacta." Although that ice cream sounded great during our 100 plus degree day, he did save me earlier from the depths of yard work hell, possible dehydration and having to deal with that witch. I told him to play the "9 and 10" exacta. We were all in!

The 10th and final race of the day went off. I never wanted something so bad for my dad. I kept on saying "nine and ten" over and over again for twenty minutes before the race. It was like a scene from the movie Rain Man. I'm sure if anyone was around us at that point they would have sworn that I had a mental issue and why was I saying 9-10 over and over like a broken record. Maybe the heat was getting to me that day?

My dad was always the guy who would give you his shirt off his back and that is why people loved him. The race started and both 9 and 10 were dead last with no show of hope. We started to walk out of Monmouth Park in shame until we heard the racetrack announcer say: "Look at this ladies and gentlemen, a late surge is brewing from the back, 9 and 10 are neck and neck coming to the final stretch!"

It felt like we were on an episode of the Twilight Zone. We looked at each other for a second and then we started to run back to the track as fast as we could. I was told that my father was a fast runner and that day proved to me that he could have given Olympian Carl Lewis a run for his money. When I finally caught up to him, to our surprise, 9 and 10 were coming down the final stretch about seven horse lengths ahead of the group. My father's last $2.00 dollars only allowed him to bet a 9 and 10 exacta not a 10 and 9 exacta too. At one point, it felt like we were running with the horses down the stretch. That's because we were!

I never screamed so loud for a horse race in my life. "Come on 9-10! Come on 9-10!" The 9 and 10 horses crossed the finish line but no one at the race track knew who had won because it was a photo finish. We had to wait 10 minutes until the officials announced that 9 had won and 10 came in second. I think we were the only people shouting for joy in the whole park that day. Who in their right mind would have played the 9-10 exacta? Us! I had never seen my father look at me the way he did at that moment. "How did you know? How were you able to do that?" I replied, "I picked nine and ten because I was nine years old once, I was just 10. That's how simple life was back then. I really didn't have to think much about anything.

My father won $793.00 off a $2.00 exacta bet. He turned to me and said, "How much do you need for your bike?" He handed me two clean crisp one-hundred-dollar bills. That was more than I needed, but he gave it to me because he really appreciated our venture together. At that moment, I realized that life is not always easy. Sometimes you have to be lucky, in the right place at the right time. But you have to be in it, to win it. Most of all, you have to be a little crazy.

I took away a few valuable lessons that day. Go with your gut instinct and luck will come your way if you ask for it. My father had a whole other respect for me. Oh, by the way, I bought my bike and never had to work for that witch ever again or drink that nasty hose water. Later that night, my father took us all out for a seafood dinner at Surf Club in Long Branch. That was where the local wise guys would hangout. That is where you went if you won big at the Racetrack. Winner, winner, lobster dinner!

Sports are in My Blood

Cap League Baseball, Chris Holtzer, RG Presley, Matt Baker, Chris O'Rourke, Johnny Avalone, Chris Crowell, myself and Jordy Ashe

I played football, baseball, basketball, tennis and golf ever since I was a child. But, one winter I was just counting the days for the Little League Baseball season to begin. I needed something to do. So, I went out with my friends, Johnny Avalone and his cousin Larry Florida, to play a game of ice hockey on Takanassee Lake. That was the only lake around that would freeze and we used to have some great hockey games there. We all knew that one area of ice was thin and would never freeze over. Johnny started to chase after a rouge hockey puck near the thin ice. I shouted, "Johnny! No, don't go there!"

Johnny fell through the thin ice and went into the freezing water. I acted quickly and grabbed his jacket and pulled him back up onto the surface. But, while I was saving Johnny, the ice around me broke and I fell in. As I went under the ice I could not believe how cold it was. It seemed like all my muscles went weak and I was not able to float. Suddenly, I felt a hand grab my shoulder and a force pulling me up. If it wasn't for Larry Florida pulling me out, I would have never made it out of that frozen pond that day. To this day, we never told our parents. We kept that a secret for over 40 years, until now. Sorry Mom. That was the first time that I almost died. Thank you Larry Florida.

I was so glad when baseball season began. My father helped me with baseball. That was the only time we had together because he worked all the time. He only had the weekends off and he loved to just sit down on his couch and watch sports on television. I didn't blame him, since I knew he worked so hard and needed rest. My father loved baseball. He really wanted me to be a pro baseball player, not football.

I was very lucky to have him coach me. My father was a true athlete, who had signed with the Kansas City Athletics MLB's American League. My father took baseball seriously. One day he was hitting ground balls to me. The ball hit a rock and then it flew into my eye. I was dazed and saw stars for a few seconds as I fell to the ground and then looked up to the sky. My father ran over to me, picked me up and brought me inside the house. He rushed to the refrigerator, pulled out a big steak and placed it right on my eye. I remember thinking how cool was that? I had no idea that a rib eye would help my eye.

He looked at me and said: "Listen, this is what happened. You were at the park playing baseball, these kids came over and took your bat. When you asked for it back, you got into a little fight. Then you say; "Mom, you should see their faces. I took all four guys on and beat them up good, and I got back my bat." I looked at him confused. My father smiled. "That sounds like a better story than I didn't keep my eye on the ball so now I have a black eye!" My father always had a way to cheer me up and make me laugh.

We had a big game against IAMA, which stands for Italian American Memorial Association. My team, the Elberon Elks Little League, was playing in the Tri City Championship. It was the best out of seven, just like the real-World Series. We had split three games apiece, and this was the final game of the championship. We were up by one run in the bottom of the ninth, two outs and bases were loaded. Peter Newman was pitching the game of his life but his arm was getting tired.

We had the greatest coach of all time. His name was Rich Braun. Coach Braun was a leader of men. He was the most respected coach and it was a real honor and privilege to play baseball for him. His knowledge of baseball and strategies were second to none and he was the coach for the Elks Club for over ten years before I got there. When we took the field for the final ninth inning, coach pulled me and Vinny Fiore aside, Vinny played short-stop and I played third base. Coach Braun said "This game is going to come down to you two. Either you, or you, are going to make the play of your life. Peter's getting tired and we need defense." Coach was right. Pete Newman was tired and was getting rocked. Vinny made two diving plays to get two outs. Vinny was super human at shortstop. Vinny should have been a major-league baseball player.

My mother took this photo of me on the far right with my hands on my knees playing third base, seconds before I made the play of my life to win the game.

It was getting so dark that the umpire almost called the game. If he did, there would have been a riot between neighborhood families. I'm not kidding. Baseball was like a religion in our area. Even Monsignor Bradley took off from church to watch the game. Over 100 plus people were in attendance and everyone was on edge. The bases were loaded and there were two outs and the count was two balls and two strikes. Then their batter hits a screaming shot down the third baseline, I dove for the ball and it shot into the web of my glove.

Coach Zambrano gave the sign to hit away with bases loaded. My father was standing only 10 feet away from third base. When I tagged the base for the final out, I just kept running into the arms of my father who then hugged me with joy. The whole team piled on us and we won the Tri-City Baseball Championship in Long Branch.

I must've practiced that play over a thousand times.

I'll never forget the coach of IAMA coming up to me after the game. His name was Paul Zambrano. Coach Zambrano was an exceptional coach who won several Tri-City Championships in his long career as a little league coach. He put both of his hands on my shoulders and said; "Son, that was the greatest play I have ever seen a third baseman make at your age. Congratulations." Paul became the Mayor of West Long Branch and is a highly respected leader in our community. He won my vote!

Can someone please find me a cheese burger! How skinny was I?

Me playing for the IAMA Babe Ruth Team

To me, Coach Zambrano saying that to me was like Billy Martin telling me I was a great player. I'll never forget that moment. I was so moved by his gesture that I joined the IAMA baseball team for Babe Ruth the next year and I had an amazing baseball experience with them.

We celebrated our win for several days. We had one pool party thrown for us after another. People were giving us free food and drinks at the Windmill Restaurant. You'd think we won the World Series the way that people were treating us after that game. That was one of the greatest summers ever. We didn't have a worry in the world. We would all go to the beach until the afternoon and then all meet up at Vancourt Park for a pick-up-game of baseball. We rode our bikes until dusk always looking for the next adventure. I was even getting more lawns to cut in the neighborhood on the weekends. It was a great feeling and I didn't want it to stop. We lived in a real neighborhood, where people cared!

Now I knew how winners felt and it was a wonderful feeling.

Meeting a Legend: Mickey Mantle

My Mickey Mantle signed Baseball

I continued to play baseball in middle school and through my freshman year in high school. I led the team in hits and we were Long Branch Middle School champions in 1981. At Babe Ruth, Long Branch, I led the league in base hits and had the highest batting average at .418. I moved from third base to the outfield and won the Golden Glove Award for my defense.

My dad was the assistant coach at the time. I'll never forget the time he took me out of a game. One of my teammates kept on throwing his bat in anger after he got an "out." So, my father made a new rule that if anyone threw their bat, they would be benched. I had struck out and as I was walking back to the bench, I tossed the bat to the fence, as all baseball players do, and my dad benched me. The team was stunned but I understood why he did that. You see, he figured, if the coach would bench his own son, it would bring order back to the team. My father's plan worked and he created a team that became a family. We won that season because no one was bigger than the team. A great lesson. Thanks Dad.

During my freshman year at Long Branch, I led the team in base hits and ended with a .620 batting average. But, that was the last year I ever played baseball. I was so excited to play football and I knew it was my ticket to get a great college scholarship. That summer, I put away my bat and glove and traded them in for some new footballs and Adidas spikes. We went into Skip's Sports, a local sports store that was owned by my father's great friend Skip Longenberger. Skip was one of my biggest supporters. He used to order my shoes and sports equipment that no other kid in town had. Don't forget, we didn't have Amazon, eBay or online buying. We had Skip and it took weeks to get our stuff, and when it came in we were happy to have it. Skip was a great man who has left a huge legacy in Long Branch.

Although I decided that I was not going to play baseball again, I still loved the game and all the great players. I was excited when my father and I went to a baseball card show and I got to meet Mickey Mantle. It was 1982 and I was 15 years old. My father mentioned to Mickey Mantle that his cousin was Rocky Colavito. Rocky was an MLB player who played with the Cleveland Indians from 1955 to 1968 and he played with Mantle for the Yankees in 1968.

That's when Mantle brought us to his private room and signed a few items for me. I only had a beat up used baseball that was tattered. Mantle looked at the ball and said, "What the hell is this son? You beat the crap out of this ball! You want me to sign this? Did you hit this ball with a hatchet?" Mantle laughed and looked at my dad and then back to me, and said "Give me the ball."

As Mantle is signing my beat-up baseball, he turned back to me and said, "Do you see this special mark here? I only make that mark when I know that someone is not going to sell their ball. You see son, this ball has meaning for you." I nodded my head in agreement. Then Mantle took out his wallet and handed me $20. "Go out to the show and buy one of my cards and you keep those two together." I took the $20 and thanked him. I bought a 1966 Mickey Mantle mint condition baseball card that day.

Joe Di Maggio, Mickey Mantle, Ted Williams, Duke Snider, Hank Aaron and Stan Musial.

Both Mickey's baseball card and his baseball are under lock and key. Those items, along with my father's Vietnam War medals, are my most prized possessions.

Every baseball I own is signed by that player in front of me, and I shook their hand. Joe DiMaggio, Duke Snider, Stan Musial, Hank Aaron, Ted Wllllams, Whltey Ford, Johnny Damon, Derek Jeter and Robinson Cano. Each of those baseballs has a great personal story and that's what makes them so special to me.

Football and My Defining Moment

Sammy Balina, Mark Shuler, Maurice Caldwell, Myself, Ray LeBron, Coach Jack Levy, Willie Stathum, Anthony Penta, Mike DiGuilmi, and Anthony Smith in the fall of 1984

I was kicking a soccer ball and making corner kicks that were going right into the soccer net. The soccer coach, James Perri, was watching me. He was trying to get me to join his soccer and that is when my life changed forever.

Coach Ed Ray, our high school's freshman football coach, was walking nearby and saw me kicking the soccer ball. He came over to me and said, "Son, can you kick a football?" Then Coach held a football and asked me to kick it. I took a few steps back and kicked that football straight through the uprights. "Do that again boy!" Coach Ray didn't hesitate for a minute. He immediately said, "You're my new kicker. Go inside and see the equipment manager."

I had no idea what had just happened. I did exactly what he said to do and got my football uniform that day. I always knew that I wanted to play football, I just didn't know how I was going to get there. Coach Perri tried to offer me all the Gatorade I could drink if I played soccer for him. But, it was no sale. Coach Perri and I still joke about that when we see one another.

Coach Ed Ray is not with us anymore, but I know he's coaching up in

Heaven. This single person made such a difference in my life as well as many other young men at Long Branch. He gave me the opportunity to believe in myself and have the confidence to be the man I am today. Thank you, Ed Ray, I am forever in your debt. He was a leader of men.

There were two families in Long Branch that really put their mark in the sports history books at Long Branch High School. The George family and the Skove family took Long Branch athletics to the next level in the 1980's. The George family were football and wrestling champions while the Skove's dominated wrestling on a state and national level. I remember watching these guys work-out and I would learn how to be a much better athlete. Billy, Danny, Alex and Tommy George were born to be athletes. I give them a lot of credit for helping to make me who I am today. They inspired me to be better than I was. They all had natural talents and I had to work harder just to keep up. I went to school with Luke, Jude, Andrew, Thomas and Simon Skove and these guys were serious wrestling icons in our state. When you have that much talent, it rubs off on anyone who is around them. I went to school with winners. Or should I say legends!

The season of 1981, the Long Branch freshman football team went undefeated 11-0. It was the first time since the 1950's that this happened since when my dad played. My father thought I was a better baseball player than football player but my father never pushed me to make a choice. That is what I loved most about him. He never pushed an agenda on me like some of the other fathers in town.

Our undefeated freshman football team was coached by head coach Ed Ray, Donald Covin and Ed Balina. Three of the greatest coaches ever at Long Branch. They taught us how to be a family. Respecting one another and having your teammates back through good and bad times. We were a family and never did we have arguments or disagreements on or off the field. We had a brotherhood that no one could divide. We all ate together, studied together and hung out together. This was the closest I ever had to having real brothers. It was magical and that is why we were winners.

I've had the opportunity to play for some wonderful programs in my life but this team was the best. Never will I forget the love that we had for one another that season and the seasons that followed. Not too long ago, I found the certificate that was given to us by Mayor Henry Cioffi of Long Branch for this incredible feat. To go undefeated and unscored upon for eleven games is remarkable for any team. I was very proud to be part of that team and the legacy we left for Long Branch football.

After our undefeated season ended, I had an appointment to see my guidance counselor. I had some questions about the classes I needed to take to prepare for college. She didn't answer me immediately. Instead she just stared at me shaking her head as if I had just cursed at her.

Me kicking with the greatest holder I ever had, James Cattelona at Long Branch

She looked at me and said that I would never go to college because of my speech impediment. My heart stopped. I looked back at her with a blank stare on my face. I said, "Are you saying that because I have a speech impediment, I will never go to college?" She replied, "That's exactly what I am saying. You're in remedial English and you can hardly communicate with people." I replied fluently, "I'm in remedial English because you keep putting me in that class when all of my test scores are 100's and I have A's." I still remember leaving her office and walking down the hall to go to the theater class. I kept thinking, "I am going to go to college and I'll make her eat her words. No matter what, I am going to go to college." I had dyslexia and no one knew how to help me. That was why I was in remedial classes. I had to work with my mother to help solve some of my issues. She used to have to read me the questions and I would answer them with no hesitation. The problem was, I did not have her with me in school when the teacher asked me to read in front of the class. Most of my teachers thought it was my speech that was holding me back. The real issue was the fear of reading things backwards in front of my classmates. I hid the fact that I was seeing things backwards because I didn't want the kids to have another thing to make fun of me. Although this was a major issue I was suppressing, I was not going to have anyone tell me that college was out of the question.

I was determined not to let her opinion stop me. My conversation with her was the first driving force behind achieving what others said I couldn't do in education, theatre and sports. It was game time and she just woke up a sleeping giant! I got to my theater class and told the drama teacher that I was there to audition for a part in their next musical. A few of my friends and others laughed when they heard what I said. One of them asked "Why would you want to embarrass yourself?" I replied, "It's going to be pretty embarrassing after school when I knock your teeth inside your throat." The laugher stopped and I got their attention.

I didn't pay any mind to them. Instead, when my name was called, I just went on stage. I practiced the lines from the script and then was getting ready to sing. No one in that room knew that I could sing. It was the many years listening to Frank Sinatra and Tony Bennett. As I started to sing all the girls stopped talking and were shocked that I could hold a note. The guys were not happy because I was there to get the lead role and no jock had ever come into their world and succeeded. Everyone at that audition was stunned. Not only did I surprise my classmates, I shocked our drama teacher who never knew I had talent. I succeeded. The drama teacher offered me one of the lead roles of the Tinman in the musical The Wiz.

Six weeks later was our opening night. We had a sold-out house. It seemed like everyone in Long Branch was there. I began to perform and I could see the audience was dumbfounded. Most of them who knew me had not expected me to perform without stuttering. Then the moment of truth, the pinnacle of all "I told you's- I can do it moments." My guidance counselor was looking at me from the forth row with her mouth wide open as if birds could've built a nest in there. The look of sheer confusion on her face made me sing louder and clearer. I sang the song "Slide some oil to me" and I brought down the house. I received a standing ovation and the show had a brief stop as the crowd cheers were loud. That was when I knew I had found my calling. The musical theatre saved my life!

Carlo Durland, Junior Lopez, Sondra Horton and me in The Wiz at Long Branch

My guidance counselor came up to me after the show with tears in her eyes. She said, "I was never so wrong about a student in all my years in education. I owe you a huge apology. You were amazing Michael." I replied, "Thank you. Can you now help me get into a school that offers musical theater?" She said, "That is the first thing I'll do on Monday morning." She gave me a hug.

Mr. Rothstein, my speech therapist since first grade, was also there to support me. He came back stage to congratulate me. He was more surprised than anyone that I did not have a stutter problem one time during my entire performance. He asked me, "What happened?" I told him that I had learned from a music teacher, Phil Maue that when I sang or memorized dialogs, I did not stutter. My stutter came when I was thinking too fast and my thought process was faster than my speech process.

Phil had discovered that I had this talent while singing for him one day after school. We worked together for several weeks and he helped prepare me for the show. I really owe Phil for believing in me and for all the hard work he had provided. This was another moment in my life that someone saw something no one else saw and gave me the opportunity to share it with the world. I am forever in Phil's debt as well.

It was a defining moment in my life when I finally put the puzzle together and realized that I was the only one who could control my destiny and not a speech therapist. I enjoyed my time with Mr. Rothstein but it was time to fly out of the nest. I was ready to control and harness my speech demons. My mother and I were working on some new things and it seemed to be working. I was getting better grades in school and I had a lot of friends who supported me and my dreams. As the saying goes, it takes a village to raise a kid. The City of Long Branch helped raise me to be that kid.

Another unsung hero to me was my quarterback, Maurice Caldwell. Maurice inspired me to look into going to college. He and I would visit Coach Ray to get advice on writing letters to head football coaches. We were two kids wanting to make something out of ourselves. We had drive.

My First Car-Working Any Job

I had a busy schedule in high school which necessitated having my own car. It was also time for me to get any job that I could to raise money for one. I learned a great lesson from my father that inspired me to get a job. My friends were all going to the movies and I wanted to take this girl out that I liked. I asked my father for ten dollars, which was a lot of money for someone in high school back then. He replied, "Go to my room to the table next to my bed and you'll find ten dollars there." I thanked him and got the ten dollars out of his table drawer and went to the movies on a date.

The following week came and all my friends were once again going to the movies. Like before, I asked my father for ten dollars and he instructed me to go back to the same table next to his bed. When I opened the drawer, there was no money there. I looked all over and checked several times to find the ten dollars. I even took out the drawer to see if it fell in the back space. I went back to my father and told him that there were no ten dollars in the drawer. Then he said, "Well, if you put back the ten dollars I loaned you last week, then you would have had ten dollars, right?" I looked at him like a deer in headlights. What can could I say? The man was right. My father was great at teaching me life lessons the hard way.

The next day, I got a job. I began working at Mazzacco's Pharmacy. It was next to the same butcher shop we've been going to for years after church on Sundays. I worked there for several weeks. I did deliveries and got to be very friendly with the pharmacist. The pharmacist was an older gentleman who loved serving and helping people. Mazzacco's was a family owned pharmacy that everyone in Long Branch used.

The pharmacist recognized that I enjoyed talking to people. So, he put me in the front to work customer service. He had a lot more faith in me than I did with my speech issue. In a strange way, it helped me concentrate better and think about what I was saying to customers. When you deal with medicine, you need to be very careful and right on point. I knew almost everyone who would come in and all their health issues. I also learned a lot about people who tried to scam the pharmacy. They had fake prescriptions or phony insurance cards. I learned very to be careful and not to trust what someone was saying. That was against my better nature. I learned some valuable life lessons from that job.

Some of my friends knew I was working there. They wanted me to get them condoms, so I spoke to the owner and asked him if he would sell them to me at a lower cost and he agreed. I made $5.00 a box and sold them to as many as 30 guys in my high school who found out about it. I was known as the Condom King. Not the most flattering name, but it was good for my college education fund at the time. It also bought me a solid reputation with the older kids in school.

Then my friend Bryan Echochart convinced me to work at Tony's Pizza in Long Branch. Tony, better known as Chubby, hired me. He knew my parents very well and needed someone who was trustworthy to deliver pizzas in Long Branch. Chubby also taught me how to flip pies and make the sauce and dough. It was a family secret that he trusted me with.

I began to deliver pizzas and found myself in a world of hard work. I was making serious tip money. I worked for the most popular pizza place in the city. I would deliver close to 200+ pies every Friday night and that was my route. We had three delivery guys working. I would make over $300.00 on Fridays and another $250.00 on Saturdays. That was huge money in 1984.

Imagine making close to $550.00 dollars for two nights as a high school student! I was rich! Although I was making great money, my father made me save it for college. My parents did not have a college plan for me. So, I knew I had to either get an athletic scholarship or save a lot of money. I played football so I could get an education. My father would say, "An education is something that no one can ever take away from you."

My father always taught me about work ethics and the importance to make a dollar, he was very kindhearted. He knew I was working hard and saving money for college. He taught me the value of a dollar and didn't want me to ever forget how hard it was to make a living. I hated working the nights when my friends were all going out and having a great time. The experience of being independent was frustrating at times. But, it also felt good to be independent and not have to look for ten dollars in his bedroom drawer. It was liberating to me.

One day out of the blue, my father called me up and said that he bought me a car. I did not know what to say. His act was out of character for him. It was not like him to buy a big item like that without me having some skin in the game. I had just received my driver's license and he was tired of me wanting to borrow his car. Since my father worked for the Ford car dealership as a service manager, I knew he had access to some great used cars.

My father says, "I bought you a Mustang!" A Ford Mustang was like hitting the teenage lottery back in 1984. The thought of me driving a Mustang was a dream come true. I called up all my friends from the neighborhood to come over. We waited for my father to drive up in my new Mustang.

Then this Red hatchback pulled into our long driveway. I couldn't understand why my father was driving a Ford Pinto. All my friends and I were in disbelief as he drove past us. He had a huge smile on his face, as if he had pulled into our driveway with a brand-new BMW.

As he pulled past my six plus friends and me, I noticed the letters on the back of the car. It read, Mustang II. Eric started an all-out laughing frenzy that all but one of my friends joined. I had to push them to stop their laughing fit.

I never would disrespect my father. He thought he had done one of the greatest things in the world for his me. I smiled and acted excited when he handed me the key. My father said, "I had the guys put in new spark plugs, new tires and a full tank of gas. Sammy detailed it for you so it's good as new." I took the key and gave him a hug and thanked him several times. This was a big moment for my father and I appreciated the gesture.

My Red Mustang II in the background. I was sitting in my future car that was owned by a friend. I always said I would drive a Benz. I was going through my Boy Band days. Look at that hair and the fake tan. You got to love the 80's.

Another great friend of mine was Nick Massaro. We used to bowl together as kids in a league. We also played high school football and we started our first band together. Nick is an amazing musician. I have always had so much respect for how he followed his dream to play in a Rock n Roll band on the Jersey Shore. We had to contain Nick from laughing. Nick kept repeating "A Mustang Two." More of my friends started to crack-up!

I told them all to get in. I didn't want my father to know that they were all laughing at my car. I told my father that Nick had just told a dirty joke and the boys couldn't stop laughing. It was like the circus when all the clowns would fit into the smallest car ever. My father watched me pull away with all my friends stacked in like sardines. As we were driving away, Eric who is sandwiched between Nick and Ralph in the backseat said, "Nice Mustang!" Pause, "Two!" We all cracked up with laughter. It was a funny moment.

The NFL Scout

In my sophomore year, I was told by many people that I'd never play football in college because I was only 145 pounds. Again, someone was telling me "I can't do that." That drove me to the gym and got me making protein shakes. In a year, I gained 30 pounds of muscle and was kicking 50-yard field goals in practice.

I had the greatest snapper, Jimmy Callano and lineman Anthony Penta, Ray LeBron, Willie Stathum, Lionel Rawls, Mark Shuler, Tommy George and Steven Bailey. I never had a field goal blocked in High School because of my teammates.

My training was intense! I had to work harder than anyone else because I wanted to be the best. I wasn't the best athlete on the field, but I was not going to let that stop my dream. I was doing 60 sets of bleachers at our high school stadium. I also was sprinting during the dead heat of a Jersey Shore summer. I was trying to gain weight that summer but my hard training kept shedding weight off. I knew that I had to train harder than anyone else if I was going to receive a scholarship.

With every bleacher step that I ran, I was getting closer to my goal. If I couldn't get my best friend, Eric Peduto, to hold footballs for me, I would use a makeshift wooden holder. It wasn't pretty but it worked. I was kicking over 150 balls a day. That's what it takes to be a professional.

Some guys didn't need to practice as hard as I did since they had natural talent.

With Coach Jim Garrett years later

All my friends were going to the beach and hanging with the girls while I was at the football field practicing. Once again, I didn't know how I was going to be an NFL player, I just wanted it so badly that I worked harder than anyone else I knew. I always said, "Talent will take you so far. Then it was up to the person on how he practiced and refined the skills that God had given them. That is what separates a great player from a champion." That is how I got noticed by Coach Jim Garrett one hot summer day.

Jim was an NFL scout for the Dallas Cowboys. One day he was using the Long Branch field to evaluate a few NFL prospects while I was there. He watched me kick and invited me to come over to his house the next day. I had no idea who he was until I walked into his home. He had pictures of himself with Legend Jim Brown. There were also other pictures of other famous NFL people. I only had only read about or had seen them on television.

The Garrett family was known to be the Kennedy's of American football and I was with football royalty. Jim worked with me on learning and understanding the special teams. Coach was a very wise teacher and student of the game. He was very patient and did not get excited unless he felt like you were half speed. Jim loved guys who hustled and played the game with respect.

I met all three of his sons in 1985. All the Garrett boys went to Princeton University and played in the NFL. Jason Garrett was a quarterback, John Garrett was a wide receiver and Judd was a running back. We used to gather on Jim's side yard and practice for hours. Jim ran it like an NFL combine. We ate together, trained together and went over to the beach that was across the street together. It was like a brotherhood of future NFL players.

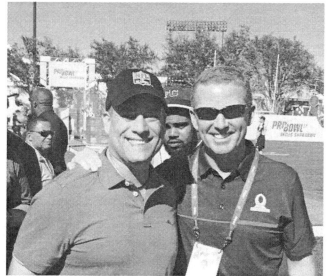
Years later, Coach Jason Garrett and Ezekiel Elliott Photo bombing us

Not only was I fortunate to play with some of top NFL players. I was honored to receive educational instruction by a legendary coach and scout. At one point, the small county of Monmouth, New Jersey had 14 active players in the NFL. We were second, only to Orange County in California. Jim Garrett made that happen. He had a special gift for locating local talent and teaching them how to take their own game to the highest level. It was magical working with Jim and his family. He inspired many players to reach their potential. I was humbled and fortunate to work with such a master of the game.

Jim made us play every position on the football field so he could give everyone a serious look. I played center to Jason, a linebacker for Judd and a defensive back for John. In return, Jason was my place holder. Judd would snap and John would run off the end waving his arms and shouting to distract me. Some of the best days of my life were spent working with the Garrett's on their side yard.

I respect my three friends who all went off to build incredible careers in the NFL. Jason backed up Troy Aikman for several years and won a Super Bowl ring. Now he's the current head coach of the Dallas Cowboys. John played for a few years in the NFL with the Bangles and got into coaching. He is currently the head coach for Lafayette University in PA. Judd played in the NFL with the Cowboys. He also played in the World League of American Football with me. He's currently the Cowboy's head of their player personnel department.

There will always be a special place in my heart for the Garrett boys. They are all still great friends of mine and I only wish them much success in their lives. These are the great guys you really want to see do well in life. A true testament to their hard work and how they were raised by two incredible parents.

Jim Garrett is the real reason why I became a prolific kicker in college and the NFL. I wasn't just kicking a football, I was positioning my kicks as a strategic planner. Almost like a game of chess, he taught me the importance of field position and what it meant to be part of the game.

These are life lessons that were never taught to me as a player. Most of what he taught us was about being able to acknowledge our instincts. Always be true to your passion and reach for the stars. Jim will always be a great leader of men.

Born in the USA and My Double Life

With Jim Simonelli, John Ward, myself, Doug Bollinger, Ed Gomez, David
Pacheco and Rubin Gomez during West Side Story.

When football season ended, I'd perform in the high school spring
musical. As a sophomore, I played the Tin Man in The Wiz. As a junior,
I played Danny Zuko in the musical Grease. Then it was the summer of
1984, which was one of the most incredible summers of my life. Not only
was I going back to high school as a senior, but it was the beginning of my
life as a young man. It was the first time that my friends and I felt a little
independent. We were all driving and excited about going to college.

That summer, Eric, Ralph, Bryan, Nick and I bought a large camping
tent and set it up in my backyard. We used to have Bryan, who was only
16, but looked like he was 25, buy us beers. With beer came girls and we
used to have so much fun. At night, we'd travel to Spring Lake, New
Jersey. We'd hang out with the girls from the theatre. We'd convince them
to tell their parents that they were staying over each other's house. These
girls never did this before. The thought of telling their parents a little lie
was exciting to them.

We, Long Branch guys, used to teach the Spring Lake kids how to live life. We had tents, beers and music. If one didn't know us, we would have looked like a bunch of red necks. All we needed was the country music and that was never going to happen. It was innocent fun.

We'd find ourselves hiding under the Spring Lake boardwalk from the beach police. They were driving Cushman golf carts and scooters to patrol the beach at night. They weren't really police. They were college students working for the summer. We had a tight click of friends who loved to hang-out together and go searching for new adventures. We used to do lip synching, play beach manhunt and have egg wars. We were all experiencing average teenage hormones when we went skinny dipping.

Bruce Springsteen came out with a new album on June 4th called "Born in the USA." Every Jersey Shore high school kid was "Boss" crazy! I remember being with my friends when I first heard his new tracks. We were at Jack's Music store in Red Bank, New Jersey, standing in line to buy it. That's what we did back in those days. We'd stand in line for days so we could be the first ones to buy a new album. Jack was pumping the music out for all to listen to. Bruce was known to stop by Jack's music store and we were hoping that our day would be that day that the "Boss" showed up. We all knew that Bruce's album was going to put the Jersey Shore back on the map after we heard it. That album was awesome. The next song was better than the first. It was Bruce's masterpiece and we bought it.

We all used to hang-out at this place called the Windmill, located on Ocean Avenue in Long Branch, New Jersey. The Windmill makes the greatest hotdogs and cheese fries in the world. It was a gathering place for several surrounding high schools. It became a territorial spot for native Long Branch guys. It was our turf and we didn't want to share it with anyone else. But, we would let pretty girls from other school's hang-out with us. We were known as the guys from the other side of the railroad tracks. A lot of them found that exciting and wanted to hang-out with us.

You see, Long Branch is known for toughness and resilience. That's because we had great football teams that dominated the Jersey Shore. We also got a bad reputation because the local Mafia ran the city and the boardwalk was their cash cow. It was a very incredible place to grow up in and I would never change anything about my hometown. The people were real, protective and fair. Everyone watched over each other and we all felt safe.

The Windmill became a sought-out destination place for high school kids to go. Kids drove from Monmouth Regional, Ocean Township, Shore Regional and Red Bank High School. Those kids would come and venture to our tough city and every time they came, an all-out brawl would happen. I never understood why it had to be that way. I'd find myself trying to make peace most of the time. I was friends with everyone and tried to avoid any altercations. I was a peacemaker.

I knew most of the football players from Pop Warner and other football camps and I was friends with them. But, some of my team members wanted to make a name and mark their territory. They wanted to kick the living crap out of anyone who came to the Windmill who didn't live in Long Branch.

Then the summer ended and the football season began. We never had a Friday night game that entire season. So, we used to hang at the Windmill for a few hours before we had to be back home for our curfew. The next day, we were playing our rival school, Ocean Township. Johnny Nies was from Ocean Township High School, he was one of my closest friends at the time because of football. Johnny was their captain, and I was the special team's captain for our team.

The Spartans came to our house for that football game waving their red towels and taunting us on the field. We played the game of our lives and we beat the Ocean Township football team 21-0. We stole a few of their red towels after the game as a great memory.

My best buddy and next-door neighbor, Eric Peduto, and I decided to stay away from the normal Windmill action. We all had a feeling that

Ocean would come and make trouble that night and all my friends were ready. As expected, a few guys from Ocean did show up and the Long Branch Police were out and ready. I did not want to lose a football scholarship over a stupid Windmill fight. Eric and I went inside the Windmill to grab a hotdog and cheese fries. As soon as we walked inside, the manager jumped over the counter and locked the door behind us. We both thought that an all-out brawl between Long Branch and Ocean was going to happen.

I remembered that we both looked towards our left as a large crowd of excited people started to run towards us. It was like the manager had announced that he was giving away free hotdogs and hamburgers. But, that was not the case.

At the same time, Eric and I turned to our right and saw why everybody was in a frenzy trying to open that glass door. The Windmill was surrounded! And, Bruce Springsteen was standing right next to me with his bass player, Gary Talent. Eric and I were like deer's in the headlights.

Bruce Springsteen was about to take a bite of his hotdog. Then he stopped and turned to us and said, "Let me buy you guys your meals for the trouble." I thought, "Did Bruce Springsteen say, I'm buying you Windmill hot dogs and cheese fries?" It was like a Hollywood movie. Then we turned around to see all our friends' faces smashed up against the glass windows. They were screaming out our names. We heard muffled screams, "Get me an autograph and you are the man, Mike!"

We didn't have social media or cell phones back in 1984. But if we did, our dinner with Bruce Springsteen would've gone viral. We would have been on every social media outlet available and known to man.

Eric's father was an authority on Tiffany stained-glass. He had finished repairing an original Tiffany piece. The piece was for Gary Talent. Eric started the conversation about his father because Gary knew Eric's father well. The Long Branch Police were coming as fast as the kids were surrounding the Windmill. The Long Branch police came right in and backed the crowd off. It took about 45 minutes for us to get out of that little glass enclosure. But, for a 17-year-old, it was the greatest 45 minutes of our lives.

Before that encounter, I had a few girls notice me, but now, I was on a whole new, higher level. I was seen eating a famous Windmill hotdog with "The Boss." Word got around quickly, not only at my school but all three of our rival schools. My senior year, I went to four senior proms. Long Branch, Ocean, Shore and Red Bank Catholic. Thank you, Bruce.

A few years later, Eric and I ran into Bruce again at the well-known Ink Well restaurant in Long Branch. We all laughed about what happened and talked about his new album coming out soon called Tunnel of Love. Right after that album came out in June, Eric and I were in my backyard talking about it. After a few beers, we were looking up at the stars and I said to Eric, "We're going to be big, like Bruce Springsteen. Write music that will change the world, make money and find a woman to love. What more can we ask for?" Then a few drops of rain hit our faces and we ran inside the tent. I'm sure that we all have had a summer like that!

The next football game I was playing at our high school stadium was a big game. It was against Neptune. During the last play of the game I kicked a field goal to secure a win for us. That's when a few guys came up to me and handed me envelopes. These envelopes had money in them. My father moved right in and took the envelopes from me. He handed them right back to those guys and said, "Don't make me call Johnny on you guys. Get the hell away from my son" What did I know? I thought it was cool that people wanted to give me money for playing a good game. I had no idea that the local wise guys were betting on our games.

I found out later in life that my father knew all about the Mob. My grandfather, Michael Sr., was involved with the Mob back in the 30s and 40s. He oversaw the golf caddies at Hollywood Country Club in Deal,

New Jersey. It was the way of life back then. Italian families helping each other with respect and honor. My grandfather, back then, was a police officer in Neptune, New Jersey. He ran a speak-easy for some "wise guys" during prohibition. He made a great living off bootlegging. I was told this story before my grandmother passed away in 1990. She even showed me the secret room that he had built in their house. It was almost like I was in the movie *Clue*.

I suppose she wanted to get that off her chest. My Grandfather had always forbidden my father to ever get involved in that world. My father also forbade me from ever getting involved with them. He was a Boy Scout, he never was arrested or got into trouble. That is why people respected him. I wanted to be like my dad and keep clean. Even when the temptation was there. God is watching!

Later, in the spring of my senior year, I played the lead role of Tony in Westside Story. I had convinced all my football teammates to become the Sharks and the Jets. Even our football coach and assistant principal, Mr. James Simonelli, became involved. He played the role of the police officer. We were the original Disney High School Musical, before that movie came out.

I was approached after one of my shows by a well-known Italian restaurant owner. He owned one of the most popular places in town visited by the local wise guys aka the Mob. He said, "Hey kid, do you want to sing in my club?" Without hesitation, I said yes. It was my first singing job. The owner made me make a promise to never tell my father and I agreed. I wanted to start being independent and this was a great opportunity of being my own man.

I started to sing in a private back room at his restaurant. It was like a Hollywood movie. Never have I seen so many beautiful women in one room. I was singing for the wise guys and their girlfriends. I sang Sinatra, Bennett and Nat King Cole songs. I was making over $1,000.00 a weekend and that was in tips. They gave me free food and even got beers for me and my friends. That was big, since none of us were legal to drink yet.

I had a great thing going on for three months until my father found out. One night I was doing my show and who walks in? My father and Johnny Donato. Johnny was a well-liked construction builder in our area. My father worked for him on a construction crew when he was laid-off from work one year. I was never so scared in all my life. You see, my father brought Johnny, to calm the club owner down if the conversation went sideways. My father was a gentle giant but if you crossed him, he would crush you.

Singing for the local Wise-Guys was a great but humble experience.

After my set ended, I sat down with all three of them. They all agreed to a deal without me even having a say about it. My father was trying to teach me a lesson on how the local wise guys can control you.

Johnny traded the owner 30 cases of wine that "fell off a truck" for me. I thought I was worth more than 30 cases of wine but I was not in a position to negotiate. This was one lesson I had to learn and there was no getting out of this one. After that night, I started singing at JR's Lounge in the Eatontown Sheraton Hotel. I was only making $100 bucks a night. A far cry from what I was making before. But it was an honest dollar and a great lesson.

Johnny and my friend Dr. Kenny Ledwitz even paid for me to make my first CD and we made 15 original big band songs. That CD helped me get a few local gigs and interest from another music producer. Johnny nor Dr. Ledwitz never asked me to pay them back for the production of that CD. It was two local guys helping another local man with a dream. I went back and sang for Johnny several times for free to show him my heartfelt thanks. Thank you, Johnny! May you rest in peace my old friend!

NITELIFE MAGAZINE • APRIL 13, 1994 • PAGE 1

MUSIC INTERVIEW
Michael Attardi and the Big Band Era

BY JERRY FERNICOLA

In the beginning... don't confuse the "Big Bang Theory" with the "Big Band Era" unless you want to consider the influence they both have on our civilization. No new young singer, composer and recording artists is influencing show business and the New Jersey Shore more than Michael Attardi. Born in Long Branch, New Jersey in 1967, Michael began his musical education as a child at home with Frances, his mother. She raised him on Cream of Wheat and the "Big Band sounds" of Count Basie, Frank Sinatra, and Tony Bennett.

Michael Attardi's strong background led to specializing in an immaculate contemporary-jazz Big Band sound, using his original own lush songs and arrangements that feature velvety brass sounds, and a "sweet" rather than "hot" approach to swing.

Michael has the triple talents of creating his own lyrics, melodies, and arrangements. He completed a debut music video called "When I'm with You" and a 7 song EP which will be released in June 1994.

Michael has just returned from San Francisco, where he recorded four Big Band originals with a 16 piece orchestra. The session was directed by the famous Jay Brower, former arranger and conductor for Perry Como, Jerry Vale and Al Martino. The project was a success.

The next big step for Michael concerning his EP project is when he returns to the studio in May to work on the final mix-downs. Michael will be working with Grammy award winner James Anderson on the engineering and mastering of the CD.

"I want to make my music as electrifying as possible by getting the most out of a classic standard or original. It's kind of like saying I compose jazz within the field of Big Band swing that I play."

I asked Michael about Mr. Anderson and how he got him to do the project. Michael replied, "Everyone in the business was telling me that Jim Anderson would never do my project because he was too busy and too big for someone like me. But, after I spoke to him and sent him my tape, Jim agreed to do my project. That had to be one of the greatest days in my musical experiences. I mean, how many artists can say that their CD is being engineered and mastered by a Grammy award winner?"

Blessed with a good strong recording voice and extremely good looks, Michael Attardi is well on his way to capturing the music world with his talents. Most of his audiences are women who simply fall in love with his baby blue eyes, let alone those who fall for his brand of "sweet" Big Band music and his romantic interpretations of the 1940s sound. Michael feels that he is making a statement and contribution at the same time. "Music for the Age of Elegance, where age is limitless and the music is timeless."

Michael has the triple talents of creating his own lyrics, melodies, and arrangements. He completed a debut music video called "When I'm with You" and a 7 song EP which will be released in June 1994.

Cover story for Night Life Magazine owned by Jerry Fernicola.

I highly respected Dr. Ledwitz and Johnny for their support. I have always said to my wife, if I was to ever make it big as a singer or writer, I would pay them back ten-fold. Dr. Kenny Ledwitz is a great friend that helped me achieve a huge goal. Thank you Doc!

Football vs. Musical theatre

I played three years of varsity football at Long Branch. I was very fortunate and will always be thankful for the great coaches and teammates that I had. Through their guidance, I became All-Shore and All County like my father. Jack Levy was our varsity football head coach and he knew his football. I had a lot of respect for that man. I used to watch football films with him and he would find the little mistakes that no one else could see. Coach Levy was a student of the game and he loved to teach football.

One of my three letters in football at Long Branch High

Coach Levy knew how to surround himself with other talented coaches. Our defensive coordinator, Bob Biasi, should have been a big time college football coach. Coach Biasi was a defensive genius and made our most talented guys look amazing. His defensive schemes are still used today and no one knows how to counter them in high school. I hold all my high school coaches to the highest level of professionalism. They were all leaders of young men. That is a gift. I know I can speak for all my teammates when I say that we were lucky to have these coaches and the support from our local community. Long Branch is one incredible city.

I also had a kicking coach. His name was Pat Sempier. Pat was so dedicated. He would drive all the way down from North Jersey and work with me, John Nies and Greg Montgomery. My uncle Pat Clay, would hold footballs for us and was always very supportive. Pat Sempier could locate talent in New Jersey and make them better. Several of Pat's students received full ride athletic scholarships in college and made it to the NFL. They were a true testament to his superior coaching techniques.

With Vivian Tomaine, my lifelong friend during Grease at Long Branch.

My graduation picture in 1985 in front of the old Long Branch High School.

When I graduated high school, I performed in summer theatre in Spring Lake, New Jersey. I was with my best friends Eric Peduto, Nick Massaro, Brian Echochart and Ralph Garry. We were known as the "Fav Five." It was our little gang of guys that were born on the other side of the railroad tracks.

Long Branch was considered the ghetto if you were from Spring Lake.

That did not bother us since the kids in the theater were cool and never treated us like that. They all treated us with respect and never made us feel like we were the poor kids from the wrong side of town. Only some of their parents and the people who ran the theater did. The Spring Lake kids had to sneak out and cover up that they were hanging out with us. In a weird way, we helped them realize that all the negative stories they heard about people from Long Branch were not true. These were great kids and most of us are still incredible friends today.

Center with Michele Sexton (former Miss Jersey) and the cast and crew from OKLAHOMA in Spring Lake, New Jersey

Spring Lake was known as the Irish Riviera to locals. Some of the richest families in the United States still live in this small town on the Jersey Shore. The Spring Lake Theatre was run by a local socialite who did not want us there. If it wasn't for Phil Maui, a former Long Branch music teacher and Adreian Burke, we would have never had that magical opportunity. I played the role of Curry in Oklahoma and Jesus in Godspell. I also played the role of Danny Zuko in Grease for the third time in my acting career.

Then it was time to start college. I had football scholarship offers from Maryland, Delaware State and the University of Connecticut. I decided to

I used to hold 7 school records in kicking for Kutztown University

go to Kutztown University after I spoke with Hall of Fame player Andre
Reed. He said, "Mike, do you want to be a small fish in a large lake or
the biggest fish in a small pond?" Andre was right. I was a place-kicker.
A 40-yard field goal is a 40-yard field goal on any football field. You get
noticed by making a lot of field goals and making the All-American teams.
I started all three years, breaking seven University kicking records, All
American Honors, All ECAC and All PSAC teams. Andre was spot on and
I had an incredible experience at Kutztown University.

At Kutztown, I continued to live a double life. I was a Thespian (I know
what you're thinking! It's kind of a funny word to describe someone in
theater) in the spring and a football player in the fall. In musical theater,
I played the roles of Amos Hart in Chicago, Marco in Carnival and J.
Pierpont Finch in How to Succeed in Business Without Really Trying.

All three musicals were smash hits! I was also able to convince a few
football players to join the cast and crew. I bribed them with meeting hot
women and it worked! Those guys thank me to this day. In fact, my friend
married a thespian. (Did I make you smile again?)

I have been very blessed and fortunate to work with so many talented people in my career. Some great, some not so great. With all of the adventures and experiences I have had in the theatre, one person always

I played Amos Hart in the hit musical Chicago at Kutztown University

was the cream of the crop. Her name was Anne Sayre and she was amazing. I'm sure you have had that feeling of being around someone who was special. Our professor Dr. Gene Huber, called me into a meeting and said, "Wait until you see what walked into my office today. This girl is smart, funny and very pretty." That was a lot coming from Gene. I met Anne during the audition of How to Succeed in Business Without Really Trying. I watched Anne auditioned from the audience and after she was

Working with a theatre group in New Jersey in the show Grease as Danny Zuko.

Anne Sayre and Me after one of my NYC gigs at the Super Club

The letter of invite to work with acting coach legend, Uta Hagen

done singing Gene turned to me and said, "I told you she was special." I shook my head with agreeance. Anne wasn't pretty, she was beautiful!

Anne received the role of Hedy La Rue, the seductive mistress of the boss and to my character. Anne is the kind of actress that helps any actor step up their game. I was a junior at Kutztown University, learning how to be a better actor from a freshman. I was humbled and inspired at the same

With Actress Anne Sayre in How to Succeed in Business

As Cinderella's Prince in Stephen Sondheim's Musical Into the Woods.

time. Anne made me a better actor that year. I always knew that she would do something big in our field. Anne spent several years on the soap opera *As the World Turns*. I am still hoping that one of these days I will be able to direct her in a film. Hint, hint! I hope you're reading this Anne?

Then on March 12, 1987, a dream came true for me. That was the day that I began working with the world famous acting coach, Uta Hagen from the HB studios in New York City. I first met Mrs. Hagen when she came to Kutztown University. She was there to teach a selected group of acting students in special one on one sessions. Never in my wildest dreams did I ever think I would be working with Uta Hagen.

Mrs. Hagen stayed for over a week. A week later, I was invited to New York City by my acting teacher, Dr. Gene Huber. Dr. Huber was writing a book about "The American Musical Theatre." He was working with American Musical legends, Stephen Sondheim and Hal Prince.

With our punter, Jeff Reifinger at Kutztown University

When Dr. Huber and I arrived in New York City he surprised me. He said we had to walk to a brownstone near Central Park. Then he told me that Stephen Sondheim owned it. I assumed he was teasing me. He knew that Sondheim was my ultimate favorite musical theater master in the world. I used to role play in a mirror to what I would have said to Sondheim if I ever had a chance to meet him. Dr. Huber was a joker and I thought this was one of his foolish pranks. I was preparing myself to see someone like Carrot Top, not Sondheim.

When we walked into the Brownstone there were several board games on tables. I asked Dr. Huber what they were. He told me that Sondheim was an inventor of board games and major toy companies wanted to buy his patents. I was going along with the joke. As I looked around the room, I saw photos of Sondheim with Bernadette Peters and Barbra Streisand.

My heart started to race and I started experiencing a cold sweat. I said, "Is this a joke or are we really in Sondheim's house?" Gene smiled and said, "I told you that one day you would meet Stephen. He called him Stephen like he knew him for a hundred years and they were tennis partners. I was still in disbelief that I was going to meet one of the most important men in the history of musical theater. This was like meeting Mozart back in the day. Better yet, hanging out with Walt Disney.

We approached Sondheim's library and saw the same barber chair from the hit musical "Sweeney Todd." in the middle of the room, inviting anyone to sit in it. I asked Dr. Huber if I could sit in the iconic chair and he said yes. Just as my butt hit the seat of the chair, I heard someone say, "Many men have died in that chair." I jumped out of the chair and turned around and saw Stephen Sondheim walking into the room.

Football was my love and the theatre was my mistress at Kutztown University.

He came over to me and shook my hand. "Hello, I'm Stephen, and you are?" That was one time that the cat had stolen my tongue. I said, "Hi, I'm Stephen it is nice to meet you." Sondheim looked at me with a puzzled face. He replied, "Gene, I thought you said his name was Michael?" Gene replies, "It is. He's very nervous right now and forgot his own name."

Sondheim laughed and asked us to follow him into his study. The only thing that was going through my head at that moment was, "I can't believe I said my name was Stephen! How stupid can I be?"

Stephen was a kind and caring man. He was very interested to learn that Dr. Huber's prize musical theater male student was a football player. I sang for him and he opened up about his passion for musical theatre and why he loved it so much. That was the greatest two hours of conversation listening to a man of pure genius. I couldn't believe that I was so fortunate to have the opportunity to have lunch with him. That was my experience with one of the greatest musical theatre icons of our time. A moment I will cherish forever.

A few days later, I was scheduled to play in the spring "Maroon and Gold" football game. My coach was not happy because I missed two practices because of the theatre and my New York City trip. During our Maroon and Gold spring football game, we ran a fake field goal and I caught a 28-yard touchdown pass. Not good if you're a kicker. I mean, kickers are not supposed to score touchdowns, only kick field goals, and the defense was not happy. Our defensive coach was screaming so much that we all thought that he was going to have a stroke. His overreaction embarrassed our defense. Then the game turned a little dirtier than expected. We had several fights between us and many cheap hits and penalties. Not good for an inter-squad team game.

Later in the game we went out for another field goal attempt. Our defensive captain was embarrassed by my touch down and acted out against me. He came full force at my blind-side and took out my left knee. It was almost like I was in slow motion. I saw him coming, but I did not have any time to react because of his speed. It was that fast. I was immediately rushed off the field by our sports medicine director Rennie Sacco.

Rennie was awesome. He knew exactly what to do and acted fast. We packed my knee with ice and then he made a few calls for me to see a specialist nearby. When my father came into the training room he was very upset. He saw the cheap hit that I received. He wanted our captain to be suspended. I told him to drop it and let's just concentrate on getting me better for the season. I blamed the coaching staff more than my teammate.

I met with Dr. Grossman in Shrewsbury, New Jersey and I underwent scope surgery that week. The surgery was a success but I slipped into a small depression during rehab. I had a lot of things going in my head. Why did my friend, our captain do that? We had also lost Coach George Baldwin that season to retirement. I had more unanswered questions than I did answers. That's when I decided to transfer from Kutztown to Montclair State in New Jersey. I needed time to heal and get over my depression.

Along with spending time to heal, I also coached some kickers. One of them was V.J. Muscillo, who went to Penn State on a full ride. I was very proud that he broke all five of my high school football records at Long Branch. Records are made to be broken and if it was anyone, I was happy V.J. did it. V.J had natural talents and was a great kicker. I had a lot of respect for him because he traded football for a higher education. He played for legendary coach Joe Paterno at Penn State. V.J is now the current Principal at Long Branch High. He helps carry on the tradition of Long Branch Football and the higher level of education to our local student-athletes of the Green Wave.

Defying Death Once Again

Singing with my Big Band at Monmouth University

After my Junior year of college, I found a few singing gigs on the weekends. I went home and got a great paying job as a roofer. Hot Tar roofing in the summer on the Jersey Shore is a suicide mission. That is why it paid $20 an hour. That was big money for a college student back in 1989 and I was saving for a new car.

I met Bobby and Jimmy that summer while I was surfing at West End beach after I trained and kicked. We immediately became friends and we liked going surfing almost every day. I always felt that swimming was a great workout and if I could add in surfing, it was a win, win.

There is one hot day that I'll never forget. My new friends Bobby and Jimmy and I headed to the beach to go surfing. When we got there, we saw a warning sign about "Red Tide." To us it was a code word for no one will be in the water and we'd get all the waves to ourselves. The three of us surfed for several hours, catching one better wave than the last with no one to get in our way. It was awesome!

The next morning, I woke up with a bad headache that was crushing my skull. I crawled on my hands and knees from my room to my parents' bedroom begging them for help. When my father saw the condition that I was in, he immediately picked me up and carried me to his car and drove me right to the ER. I was seen by several doctors who could not explain what I had or how to ease my severe head pain.

I went blind for an hour and could not hear as well. My body was shutting down. The only way I could communicate was by blinking my eyes twice for yes and once for no. A specialist came into my room and preformed a spinal tap. The spinal tap confirmed that I had viral meningitis of the brain.

I found out that Bobby and Jimmy were also in the same hospital at the same time. Bobby, Jimmy and I were all fighting a battle to save our lives. We spent two months in the hospital recovering. I never saw Bobby or Jimmy after that experience in the hospital. I tried to look them up but I never got their last names. I guess I thought I would see them again.

Monmouth Medical Center was great. They saved my life. The staff was friendly. The nurses and doctors were class A. They knew exactly how to treat my illness and got to work on me right away. I was lucky. My parents were scared but I had a feeling that everything was going to be fine, and it was. I prayed a lot during those days. It was the only thing I could do to keep my spirits high. I knew that God was there.

My Aunt Donna and Uncle Pat visited me one night and handed me a card. In the card was a poem. It told the story about "Footprints." In short, a man is walking on the beach in the sand and see two sets of footprints. He notices that Jesus was walking with him every step of his life. He always saw two sets of footprints through the good times.

Then a tragedy happens and the man is in a bad way. The man turns to Jesus and says, "You were with me during all the good times in life. But, when I needed you the most, you abandoned me and left me to fend for myself." Jesus replies, "When life was hard and you only saw one set of footprints, I was carrying you." WOW! That put it all in perspective. I was ready to get back to my life and follow my dreams once more. Thank you,

Jesus, for carrying me through my toughest times.

I remember telling myself that I feel great! I knew I would beat this viral meningitis. I was going to walk out of that hospital someday healthy again. And, I did. We all recovered. That was the craziest summer I ever had. I almost died for a second time in my life. Thank you, God!

Capitol Hill and Broadway Calls

My junior year of college with my parents.

The summer was almost over and I was at home healing. At that time, I also began helping a family friend, Frank Pallone, Jr. to run for U.S. Congress. The first-time congressman was Frank Pallone, Junior. Frank loved the environment, and so did I. I almost died from "Red Tide" ocean pollution. It was my mission to make a difference. It was also my mission to help get Frank elected. I knew he would try to help stop those who were killing our ocean environment.

Since I was an English major and Political Science minor, I wanted to write speeches for Frank. I worked on his campaign and oversaw his college absentee ballots. I canvassed the state of New Jersey and set up Democratic clubs at every college in New Jersey. I wanted to help preserve our environment and I felt my own personal story could lend value to a serious issue we were facing in New Jersey. Frank was on a mission to stop ocean dumping and took on several huge companies to stop the pollution.

We lived in a Republican area and getting Frank elected was a shot in the dark. Yet, Frank won that election by a few thousand absentee votes.

He became a first-time Congressman in 1988. Frank was so thankful that he took me to Washington D.C. that year and I worked on Capitol Hill as an intern. At one point, I could not believe I was there in our nation's capital working for an elected U.S. Congressman. And, I knew he was going to make a difference.

During that time, I was awarded the LBJ Scholarship grant. Then I studied at the University of the District of Columbia. It was a predominantly African-American college. I studied English and political science for a semester. It was a wonderful experience and I loved being there. During my first class at the university, I was taking African-American poetry. I was the only white person in the whole entire class. Our instructor was the famous African-American Poet Mrs. Julia Fields. Mrs. Fields said, "I want everyone to write a poem as if you were a slave during the Civil War."

I felt like I was in an "EF Hutton" T.V. commercial when every student's head turned towards me. Never in my life did I ever feel like a minority until that moment. You could hear the crickets outside as the silence filled the air in our classroom. It drew the attention of Mrs. Fields. She began to laugh outload as she walked over to me. Julia put her hand on my shoulder and said, "You can write about how you were a slave master Mr. Attardi." The whole class broke out in laughter. Even I was relieved to know that she had a great sense of humor. That was one of my best classes ever in college. I learned a great deal from Julia Fields. She also played a big part in making me into a prolific writer and songwriter.

The months that I worked on Capitol Hill were also remarkable. I had the opportunity to work with Congressman Joseph P. Kennedy, son of Robert Kennedy. Congressman Kennedy was working on an environmental bill. I volunteered to do the research on several key issues. The bill passed into law and I learned a great deal about carbon law and garbage incineration. I also worked on Senator Bill Bradley and Lloyd Benson's re-election campaigns.

The highlight of my Washington, D.C. experience was a luncheon I had with Senator Edward Kennedy. We had lunch during a young Democrats Day at the Capitol Hill Cafe. Having Lunch with a Kennedy was a dream come true for any political science major in college. I sat only two seats away from Senator Kennedy. He was gracious and he even signed a photo I had of him.

I was raised a Kennedy Democrat, a moderate who voted for Reagan, (in secret). If they ever knew I voted for Reagan, I would have been sent home to New Jersey. But, I always voted for the person, not the party. Politics has hit an all-time low by anyone's standards today. So, I'm a mid-conservative voter. Lately, swinging more to the right side of major issues.

My claim to fame on Capitol Hill was creating a new bill for Frank to introduce to the House of Representatives. The idea came to me after watching the movie Scarface with Al Pacino. I asked the question of to where or to whom does all that money go after the government seizes it? After weeks of research, I found that the money was turned over to the U.S. Attorney General. Some of that money was being used to build nicer prisons. You know, the prisons for the rich and famous with golf courses and bowling alleys.

Frank felt that it was far more important to use that money for another purpose. He wanted to use it to rehabilitate and teach people about the harm that drugs can do. He wanted to allocate money to reinforce the law agencies who were fighting the drug lords. The bill passed into law. I left Washington DC in December 1990 with wonderful memories.

In 1989, I started my football training again in New Jersey. We were training for the upcoming spring football season at Montclair State University. A week after I began training, I received a call from an old friend, Gene Huber from Kutztown University. Gene and I talked. During our conversation, he convinced me to audition for a Broadway show. It was called Starlight Express by Andrew Lloyd Weber. The show ran on Broadway for over four years and they wanted to take it on the road.

I traveled into New York City and auditioned. I had an incredible time singing and skating. I had the advantage over some of the other actors because they didn't know how to skate and I did. I used to be on the speed racing skate team at Eatontown skating rink. It was one of the first times I ever kissed a girl at that skating rink.

To M.K., Edward M. Kennedy

A few days after my audition, I was cast and made the tour show. I had to make a choice. Was I to follow my dream of someday playing in the NFL or take a job skating around and singing in a real Broadway show? This was the crossroads I always knew would happen, I just didn't know when. I was not willing to trade my spikes for skates yet. I went back to Montclair State University. I finished my senior year playing football there.

My sisters Francine and Michelle during my Junior year of college

ACT II
Hello- Joe Di Maggio, NFL and Japan

I played one year of college football at Montclair State University. Then in fall 1990, I sprained my left ankle the first day of summer football camp. I had to wear a soft cast for the entire season. Coach Rick Giancola had a lot of patience with me. One day he came out to hold for me during practice. More than likely, it was the first time he had done that since he played football. Coach was trying to get my confidence back and he knew that his gesture was well received. I made all my field goals during the next game against Hofstra University and we were on our way to the finals. Unfortunately, we lost against power-house football college Union. They went on and won the Stagg Bowl that year.

Even with a sprained left ankle, I made the All NJAC and ECAC Teams. But, every NFL scout that was following me at Kutztown, seemed to fade away. Fortunately, Jim Garrett, who was scouting for the Dallas Cowboys, called me. Jim told me that he would bring me in after the draft.

I had several un-official kicking workouts with Coach Garrett. In fact, his son Jason Garrett, used to hold footballs for me during my several kicking workouts. I found myself once again in the Garrett's side yard. This field hosted some of the greatest Jersey Shore football players. Every one of Coach Garrett's players invited to practice in his side yard, made it into the NFL, CFL or World League. Some of those who made it included: All three of his sons-Jason, John and Judd, his son-in-law-Harry Flattery, Charlie Rogers, Sam Mills, Greg Montgomery, John Nies, Ken Hill, Danny Stubbs, Tony Racioppi, the Christian brothers, and some of the greatest college players from the Jersey Shore.

On October 1, 1990, I signed a contract with the World League of American Football. That used to be a farm league for the NFL, owned by several NFL owners. I traveled to Sacramento, California with several kickers. I kicked there for only three weeks before I went back with the

Los Angeles Raiders that spring. My friend Johnny Nies kicked for the Sacramento Surge and that is what got him with the Buffalo Bills. We were two kids from the Jersey shore trying to make it into the NFL.

Kicking at Montclair State University with Coach Pat Sempier

Before I went to the Raiders in 1991, I worked for Former NFL player, Kenny Hill at Pro to Go, Inc. I needed to make money and the opportunity sounded like fun. I oversaw the booking of New York Giants players on special events. It was an awesome job for someone who was trying to make the NFL. It allowed me to meet some interesting guys. If you were a Giants fan as I was, it was a dream job come true. That was the same year of Desert Storm and the Gulf War.

The NFL did not want to do the big hoopla due to the nature of wartime. A formal MVP trophy was never presented to Otis Anderson. He never experienced that huge honor the way it was celebrated in the past years. Giants fan's felt bad for Anderson, but his day would come shortly after.

Waterford Crystal's CEO was a family friend, Billy George Senior. Mr. George knew I was working with Otis and contacted me. He wanted me to help his company present a Waterford Crystal trophy at Macy's, Herald Square in New York City. With his deep raspy voice Billy said, "Mikey, I want you to do me a favor. We've been trying to get this MVP Waterford trophy to Otis Anderson. Can you help me Mikey?" I would have done anything for Mr. George. I had so much respect for him and his family. The George family had always treated me with respect and the thought of helping Mr. George was a true honor. I replied, "Mr. George, it would be an honor to help you. I will call Otis right now and make this happen."

As Mr. George was presenting Otis Anderson with the MVP Waterford Trophy, Mr. George looked at me. It was if he wanted to say something. His eyes said what he was feeling. Then he said softly, "Thank you Mikey." I smiled. Mr. George was the only one who used to call me Mikey. I kind of liked that he was the only one to call me that. Mr. George passed away a few years later due to a heart attack. It was very hard for our community who loved and respected this man. Mr. George was a hero to many of us in Long Branch. He was a coach, a teacher and a friend. He will always be missed. But, his legacy and spirit lives on in his wonderful children and grandchildren.

Kenny Hill was a former NFL Player with the Raiders and he was the person that got me my first big break in the NFL. Kenny called his old coach with the Raiders, Steve Ortmayer. Kenny's call got me back with the Los Angeles Raider's camp in 1991.

I signed with an agent by the name of Tim Kane. Tim had a few players in the NFL and represented the kicker from the Miami Dolphins, Pete Stenonovich. I flew down to Miami and worked out with Pete a few times. Pete was a great guy. Pete had a wild side to him that made him fun to be around. Pete was also the very first million-dollar kicker in the NFL. Pete set the bar for future kickers coming into the NFL.

I met Dan Marino a few times, but I didn't socialize or hang out with him like I would with Mark Duper and Mark Clayton. Marino is a great guy, but I wasn't in his league. Miami became my training ground for several cold New Jersey months that year. I loved being in Miami, that city bursts with so much life. It was a melting pot city like New York.

During the off season, I traveled to Japan in 1991 before the NFL American Bowl. I was hired to do public relations and marketing for the Los Angeles Raiders. I created a Raiderette poster that we were trying to sell in Japan before the Raiders vs. Dolphins game. We sold the poster to the Tokyo Dome and made a few bucks. We had a deal with Coke that went sideways and our posters were held up in Japanese customs only a day before the game. We lost a lot of money on that deal. That was the last time I ever drank Coke. Besides, I was never really was a fan of soda. My mother never did allow us to drink it anyway.

Years later, Otis and I showing off our bling and me holding the NY Giant's Super Bowl trophy.

During my Japan trip, I met Hall of Fame baseball player Joe DiMaggio. I had lunch with him and his sister at the Tokyo, New Otani Hotel in 1991. This is where I met George Silk who worked for Life Magazine. George shot the first pictures of Nagasaki, Japan, after the atomic bomb was dropped. He also photographed Japanese war criminals awaiting trial in postwar Tokyo.

While I was having lunch with DiMaggio, a fan came up and asked for his autograph. Joe politely responded that he would sign something after his lunch. The fan got mad and said, "So what was it like getting dumped by Marylyn Monroe?" Joe bounced up from his seat and went towards the guy. I jumped up and pushed the guy out of the restaurant as if I was Joe's body guard. Not that Joe needed me to step in, but out of respect to Joe, I handled it. I can't imagine the pain Joe was feeling at that time. Joe still had a soft spot for Monroe and anyone who disrespected her was not on his nice list. Joe did not recover well from that rude encounter and we had to cut our lunch short. It was an honor to have lunch with my Dad's hero. I finally understood what Simon and Garfunkel's lyric meant: "Where did you go Joe DiMaggio." He was a legend who personified everything good with humanity. Where has that gone?

Later that night a few of us hit the hotel bar and ran into some baseball greats. I had drinks with MLB Hall of Fame Icons: Ted Williams, Johnny Bench, Tom Seaver, Nolan Ryan, Yogi Berra and Whitey Ford. Yogi and I talked for hours. He was funny and straight to the point. He loved his country and baseball was his religion. I said to Yogi, "How was it playing with Mickey Mantle?" Yogi said, "Mickey was a great player and the life of the party. Everyone wanted to be Mickey Mantle. I've seen grown men act like little school boys when they met Mickey. And, he liked being liked. That is what made him special. He loved the fans and they loved him."

Yogi and I also talked about Montclair, New Jersey, since he lived there with his family for many years. I told him that I played for Montclair University and that is how we became drinking partners that night. I will never forget my time with Yogi. It was almost like spending time with an older and wiser grandfather. He loved to share his words of wisdom. We had many laughs and some serious moments as well. I guess it was a Jersey thing!

I learned that night that these legends were in Japan for the Hall of Fame baseball game in Tokyo. All the players signed baseballs for me that I still have in my personal sports collection.

Los Angeles was a Dream that Ended Up a Nightmare

I was with the NFL with the Los Angeles Raiders on their Practice Squad for the 1991-1992 seasons. I lived in the Los Angeles area in El Segundo for three years. During the beginning of my L.A. years, I lived with Steve Ortmayer and his family for several months. He was the General Manager of football operations for the Los Angeles Raiders.

Steve and Merylee Ortmayer were remarkable people who took me into their family. Steve has been a father-figure and has helped me make some tough choices in my life. Not only was Steve the Special Teams Coach, but a great teacher and gifted scout. He gave me a chance when others turned me away.

In Tokyo, Japan during the NFL American Bowl game in 1991 with a Dolphin Cheerleader friend.

Then I got an apartment with a high school friend, Stan "Chip" Albers, who was an actor on "All my Children" soap opera. Living in Los Angeles was no doubt, the craziest and most fast paced life I ever had. Hanging out with Keanu Reeves at the Bill and Ted's Excellence Adventures. River Phoenix before he passed away and Mickey Rourke after parties.

There were a few party nights with actor Luke Perry of "90210." I was hanging out with more actors than Raider teammates. It almost looked like I had made my decision to be an actor. An audience could assume that this was the case. One night my teammate Nolan Harrison and I had drinks with Eddie Murphy and Arsenio Hall at the Roxy. We hung out with Kathy Ireland, Cindy Crawford and other super models. Magic Johnson threw parties for the Raiders after every game at one of his clubs in L.A.

One time, my friend Chip dared me to go on a commercial audition for Miller beer. I got lost trying to find the studio for my call back. Then I saw a guy wearing a motorcycle helmet and I approached him to ask for directions. The guy took his helmet off and it was Patrick Swayze. I froze like a deer in headlights. I went on to tell him that I was with the L.A Raiders and my friend had dared me to audition for this TV commercial. Swayze told me to hop on his bike and I did. He rode me down the street in front of the studio I was trying to find. The producer for the commercial saw me getting off the bike with Patrick and walked over. They both knew one another and got into a conversation. Patrick said I was his old-time friend and I got the job. As a thank you, I gave Swayze two sideline passes to a Raiders game that week.

I shot the commercial a week later. But, the controversial Clarence Thomas trial was going on. Miller Beer decided to pull the ad because it was too sexist. Talk about bad timing. Patrick and I kept in touch during my L.A years and we hung out several times. I was crushed when I heard that he had cancer. Patrick Swayze was a great man and may he rest in peace.

Later that same year, Chip and I auditioned for a new reality show called "Studs." It's about a guy who goes on three dates and then comes back and describes what he did on the dates. The producers told me that my dates were too "Boy Scout" and they passed on my episode. The three girls were nice and I dated one of them for over a year until she moved back to Seattle. I have a lot of respect for women and I wasn't going to go on a reality T.V. show and lie. All the girls were great and we had wonderful dates. I guess, I am too much of a Boy Scout. But, why is that so bad?

Later that year I received a call to pose in GQ magazine. I was weighing in at 180 and was in the greatest shape ever. A photographer from the show Studs asked if I was interested in modeling. Of course, I said yes! Who wouldn't be? GQ was one of the hottest publications at the time. This was a once in a lifetime opportunity and I was going to make it happen.

I showed up in a Los Angeles bright white studio with flowers everywhere. Then this beautiful woman, a skinny red head, dressed in a tight yellow half dress walked into the room. The minute she saw me, she started to grab me. I was like, "Hey what's going on?" Then I heard the camera clicking. I let her take control since she was a professional and I had no idea what I was doing.

Posing for GQ Magazine in 1991

She pulled me towards her and started to kiss me as I heard the clicking of camera frames being shot. The photo that made GQ was when we separated from our kiss. At first, my heart was racing. I had never walked up to a stranger without saying a single word and start making out with them. That was a first.

Then one-night Chip and I were having dinner at Wolfgang Pucks. Then we saw the famous actor, Tony Curtis in the restaurant. It was one of my greatest highlights of my Los Angeles years. This was Tony Curtis! The actor who made out with Marylyn Monroe in the classic film, *"Some like it Hot."* That was one of my favorite movies growing up and I had it on VHS (now I'm showing my age) at the time. I must have watched that film over a hundred times. Jack Lemon and Tony were my heroes.

Chip and I were like two little school boys trying to get the other to go over to him. We did rock, paper, scissors. We did "my mother said." We even drew straws. Then he double dared me and there is no way out of a double dare.

Posing again for GQ Magazine in 1991

I got up from my chair and walked over to Mr. Curtis. "Mr. Curtis, I'm a huge fan. My name is Mike Attardi and I'm a back-up kicker for the L.A. Raiders." There were a few seconds of silence and that is when a rush of fear started to set in. This might not be such a good idea after all?

Tony Curtis says, "The L.A. Raiders? The Silver and Black! Al Davis's Bad Boys, Just Win Baby Raiders!? Holy shit son, I'm a fan of yours!

Have a seat. Can you get me tickets next week against San Francisco? Listen, if you can get me those James Garner sideline tickets, I'll get you laid, you son of a bitch! Not that you need me to get laid, you're a good-looking kid but what the hell, I'll hook you up son!"

Still to this day, I don't know how it was possible for anyone to say all that, in one breath. Holy crap! Tony Curtis was a Raider fan. I asked Tony if he would call over Chip, the same way he called Jack Lemmon in the movie Some like it Hot. You see, Chip's name is Stanley. Chip never liked being called Stanley.

Without skipping a beat, Tony stood up and looked over at Chip. Chip was still in disbelief that I was sitting with Tony. Then Tony shouted, "Oh Stanley, Stanley, why don't you join us for a cup of tea?" The whole restaurant went silent and looked at Tony. "Chop, Chop! Hurry up you fool. Time is not waiting and neither am I."

Chip got up, ran over and shook Tony's hand and then sat down next to me. I could have sworn that Chip had kicked me under the table a few times in disbelief. Seeing Chip nervous, awesome! Having dinner with Tony Curtis, Priceless!

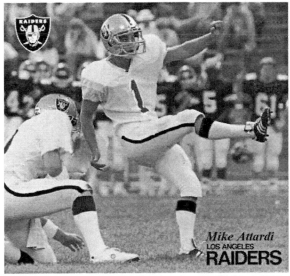

Kicking in pre-season camp with the Los Angeles Raiders 1991-1992.

After the NFL football season with the L.A. Raiders, my life was scripted like a Hollywood movie. I was hanging out with two Hall of Fame players Marcus Allen and Ronnie Lott. How much better does it get for this kid from Long Branch, New Jersey?

With Ronnie Lott, Monica and Marcus Allen

Years later Marcus Allen and I met in Arizona for a Super Bowl

The NFL stands for: "Not For Long." In the fall of 1992, the L.A. Raiders released me with a torn groin muscle. They also knew that I had lower GI issues and blood in my stool. They had to make the 52-man roster cut and I was on that list once again.

When I was released from the Raiders, I made a phone call I to Coach Jim Garrett. I wanted to tell him the news. The Coach, in his calm voice, says, "John became the new special teams coach under Coach Sam Wyche at Tampa Bay. Give John a call, I'm sure he'll look at you."

I called John Garrett at the Tampa Bay Buccaneers and he told me to come out to Tampa for a tryout. I canceled my flight to New Jersey and booked it to Tampa Bay, Florida. This might have been the opportunity I was looking for. Then again, what was I going to do about my health issues? I guess, I'll take it one step at a time. I called my parents and my agent Tim Kane and told them I was heading to Tampa Bay for a tryout with the Buccaneers. They were happy for me.

I arrived in Tampa, John Garrett met me at the Buccaneer practice field and I got changed to kick. Myself, Ian Howfield and Carlos Huerta were all there trying to make the team. I made all my field goals but came up short on my kickoffs. The NFL wanted kickoffs minus five-ten yards in the end zone. I was placing them plus 5 yards. I did not have the power in my leg at that time. I was battling a torn groin and a medical problem that I didn't understand.

John was a fair and honest person. Ever since I first met him at his father's backyard on the Jersey Shore, John and I had developed a strong bond. John was always a role model for aspiring football players who lived the area. I respected him and his ability to find talent. He was taught by the best, including his father, Jim. With that said, I had a great workout. And, they were talking about the opportunity of me to kick for the Tampa Bay Buccaneers. I had to disclose my health issues since I had so much respect for John and I did not want to put him in a bad situation.

John appreciated my honesty and released me from anymore tryouts with Tampa Bay. In a serious conversation, John told me to go home and take care of my health. This was nothing to ignore. John was right and I made plans to go back to New Jersey that night.

The flight home that night was tough for me. I had to embrace the reality that I might be sick. The thought of me traveling around the country for NFL tryouts was an exhausting thought. I called up my agent Tim Kane and told him that I needed a break. Tim did not understand at first and he felt like I was quitting. I never quit anything in my life. The thought of someone who I cared about thinking I was a quitter did not sit well with me.

I said, "Tim, I think I'm sick. I have blood in my stool." Tim replied, "What the hell did you eat? Are you eating Sushi again?" I said, "No I'm not eating Sushi. I'm sick! I have something wrong with me." Tim said, "Come home and we'll get you to see a doctor. Now you have me concerned."

When I landed in New Jersey the next day, I was not feeling right. I must have gone to the men's room several times with blood in my stool. Was it from my nerves? Was it something bad I had eaten in Los Angeles? All I know is that I did not care too much because I was excited to be home in New Jersey with my family. My father picked me up at the airport. He looked at me and said, "Are you feeling OK? You look like you lost some weight. Are you sick?" I assured him that I was feeling great because I didn't want to worry him. I was happy to be home with my family.

When I arrived at my parent's house, my mother made me a dinner that was fit for a king. My sisters, Michelle and Francine joined us and we had a great night. We didn't speak about football - why would we? We had so much more in common as a family that our conversations were fun and positive. I didn't want to be the "Debbie Downer" of the group and have everyone feel bad for me. I did share with them my concerns about my health issues and they all agreed that I needed to see a doctor the next day. My sister Michelle set up an appointment for me to see Dr. Michael Arvanitis, who is a colon/rectal surgeon. We were family friends and I wanted to see someone that I trusted.

Having to see a colon doctor is not on your top five things to do in your lifetime. In fact, at 24 years old, it was pure horror to think that someone is going to be poking around your backside. My colonoscopy was performed under much restraint and displeasure. The procedure was painless. Dr.

Arvanitis was gentle. But, the reality of another person shoving a camera inside you was nothing to write home about. Dr. Arvanitis was cracking jokes during my procedure. It made me think that if my sister set me up on a Candid Camera episode during the procedure. Who knows, maybe I would have been as famous as the Kardashians? Talk about reality T.V. before its time.

Dr. Arvanitis took some tissue samples and told me that he would call me in a few days with the results. I didn't have a worry in the world. I knew I was fine. I was doing this for my family so I didn't have to hear my mother complain that I don't take care of myself. I was only a world class athlete at the time but that did not matter to my mother. She still treated me as her little boy.

A few days later I get a call from Dr. Arvanitis. Doc said, "I want you to come in today to talk. I have some concerns." Not a good way to start a conversation I thought. I agreed and went in to see him later that day. Dr. Arvanitis walked into the waiting room with an assured smile and brought me to his office. There were several x-rays on his wall and he started to point to what looked like a large intestine. I took anatomy in college, I better know what a large intestine looks like. I said, "Is that my large intestine? And what the hell is that? As I pointed to a black mass area. Doc said, "That is your large intestine and the area there has the first stages of cancer. It's better known as severe ulcerated colitis. Your tissue samples don't look good." I turned back at him and said, "Are you kidding me? Did my sister put you up to this? Cause it's not funny." Doc replied, "It's not funny. We need to remove it before it spreads. I can get you into the operating room as soon as possible. Mike, do you understand what I am saying?" I replied, "I understand what you're saying but are you sure? How the hell did this happen? This doesn't run in my family. No one has cancer." Doc looked at me as if he knew that I needed to take a minute to catch my breath. This was a lot to take in for someone who, only a week ago, was with the Los Angeles Raiders, and the Tampa Bay Buccaneers.

When I returned to my parent's house that day, I broke the news that I had to go in for an operation. My mother and grandmother Millie started to cry. Millie took out her rosary beads and started to pray. Millie would have prayed if I had a hang nail. My sisters both hugged me and my father put his head to mine. They all were in better spirits during dinner. Then I got a phone call from Dr. Arvanitis. He said that I was scheduled to be in the hospital for my operation in a few days. He told me that I had to fast. I had to go to the pharmacy and pick up a special drink to clear out my system a few days before my operation.

I thought I was fine until I found out that I was not able to eat my mother's famous baked ziti during Sunday's family dinner. My mother made the best baked ziti and it was torture to smell it and not be able to savor the taste. There I was, drinking that nasty stuff doc prescribed. It was like drinking salty egg whites. Not that I know what salty egg whites taste like but what I imagined that nasty salty egg whites might taste like. I had to hold my nose to swallow the last few ounces. My father was getting a kick from the regurgitating reflux I was experiencing. But, he knew not to cross the line to laugh. I gave him a smile. I wanted to comfort him, knowing that he was keeping in his true emotions about what I was going through. My dad was tough like that.

A few days later, I was in a hospital gown lying on a gurney and being wheeled into surgery. My mother looked down at me with her beautiful brown eyes. She said, "God doesn't give things to people who can't handle them. You're a fighter and my hero. I love you." I smiled and said, "I love you from here to the moon and back." That was the last thing I heard before I saw Doc waiting in the operating room. It was cold in that room, I mean freezing!

When I'm nervous I start telling jokes to lighten-up the people I'm with. I guess "Your Momma" jokes weren't the proper choice of jokes to tell during that situation. Then again, when is it proper to tell "Your Momma" jokes? Several nurses were laughing and the other doctors were smiling. I could tell because their eyes were squinting over their surgical mask. The only two people in that room that weren't laughing was Dr. Arvanitis and me. Dr. Arvanitis was very focused and ready to take care of business. I had all the confidence in the world that he would do a great job. I looked at Doc and said, "You know if you screw this thing up you're going to have to deal with my mother and Michelle." He replied, "Why do you think I wasn't laughing at your Momma jokes before."

Several people surrounded my gurney as they slid me over onto the operating table. I don't remember feeling any fear as I was about to go under. Doc looked down to me and said, "You're going to be fine. You probably have taken harder hits in football then you will today. This is your anesthesiologist and he's going to make you feel good right now." I looked at the anesthesiologist and said, "Your Momma's so fat, that when she moves backwards, her butt beeps! Beep, beep." He replied, "I want you to count backwards from 10." I started to count, "10, 9, 8, 7." Then it was lights out.

With football great Joe Morris, my wife and sister at the Super Bowl.

Football was my love but Music was my Mistress!

My original CD was released in 1994

The Football season was over and I was still healing from my operation. But, I still wanted to practice kicking. I found an indoor field in New Jersey to kick. So, I began kicking and training at Goodsports. I remember practicing at that indoor football field until the wee hours of the night. I was beginning to feel sick and starting to look a little weak. But I mustered up all my courage and will-power to keep on training. No matter how I felt, I continued to train every day.

During every practice, I kicked around 150 footballs. My friend Tony Raccioppi would hold for me. Tony was an incredible aspiring NFL quarterback. He trained harder than anyone I knew. I still say that he would have been a great NFL player if he had the right agent to represent him.

I was back in New Jersey meeting with doctors about my torn muscles and my GI troubles. It was difficult. Even though I was sick I still had to find work. So, I took a job as a teacher in Long Branch High School. I also took a football coaching job with Coach George Conti at Ocean Township. Ocean Township was a rival high school to Long Branch. My friends still to this day call me Arnold, as in Benedict. We had a serious rival back then and it continues today.

One night my friends Eric, Ralph and I went out to hear a jazz band play in Asbury Park, New Jersey. At the time, I was talking to them about starting a Big Band and doing gigs. Later we all went to the Long Branch Hilton Hotel. We went there to listen to a trio that we had heard a lot about. I wanted to hear them play. These were some serious cats playing jazz and standards.

Vinnie Correa, Gladstone Trott, Chico Rouse Jr.
and Steve Swanson at the Bitter End in New York City

The trio was Gladstone Trot, Vinnie Correa and Chico Rouse Junior. Gladstone had played piano for the Count Basie Orchestra. Chico's father had played for Thelonious Monk and Vinnie had played for Ella Fitzgerald. Not too shabby for anyone's standards.

We were not disappointed in their performance. They were outstanding. Their timing and rifts were of legends. I was so impressed that I went up to Chico after the first set and asked him if I could sit in for a few songs.

Chico said for me to come back in 15 minutes and I did. But, he never did call me up to sing. I went every Friday and Saturday night for eight weeks. Every time I would ask to sit in and sing and Chico would always say to come back in 15 minutes.

I was very patient and I waited until the time was right. I am very persistent. But I didn't want to be pushy. I wanted this relationship to grow and not come to a complete stop. My patience helped my agenda with these guys. I also wanted the room to be much larger and I needed the hotel manager to be there. I waited until all the stars were lined up.

Then the ninth weekend came and I had invited several friends to come. I also made sure that the hotel manager was there. Right before the band was about to play their second set, I jumped up on the stage. I said to Gladstone, "Missed the Saturday Dance in C." Then I turned to Vinnie and said, "Slower tempo in front and jazz it up after the second verse."

Mike Attardi & his Big Band played the Bitter End for several weeks in NYC

Chico was about to kick me off the stage when I turned to him and said, "Hold the tempo behind Vinnie's solo after the chorus." Chico sat back on his drum stool and starts his drum lick after the piano intro. When I started to sing, the whole lounge area stopped talking. I felt like I was in a movie where everything around me stopped for one moment in time. The fact that no one ever sang during the band sets must have gotten the audience's attention. Not to mention that all the stars were lined up at this point.

When the song was over, we receive a huge applause. People came up to me to request songs like, It had to be You and Fly me to the Moon. I noticed a few wise guys from back in the day there. It was almost like the protocol son had returned home and was being welcomed with open arms.

One older Italian man came up to me and asked, "You're Mike Attardi's son. You used to sing for us in the back room a long time ago. Remember me, Frankie." I responded, "How can I ever forget you Frankie, you were my best tipper." If you said that in front of their wives or their "Comara" (It's Italian slang for "An on the side girlfriend) you'd receive a bigger tip.

The manager of the Hilton came over to us and said, "What the hell was that? It was amazing! You never told me you had a singer Chico? Chico replied, "We've been saving him for a rainy day. Besides, our contract is up." The Hilton manager replied, "I'm going to extend your contract and add in more money for the kid to sing." Chico shook his hand and made the deal on the spot.

Chico turned to me and said, "Why didn't you tell me you could sing, Bro?" I replied, "You never asked Bro!" He said, "You come up to me stuttering asking me to sing. How the hell did I know you were like Mel Tillis!" I said, "You should never judge a book by its cover." He replied, "I didn't understand what the book was about. Damm! You can sing boy! Now you're gonna sing for me!" Chico put his arms around me and gave me a strong man hug.

They made more tips that night than all summer nights combined. We had a meeting later that night and agreed that I would look for gigs for our new group in New York City. That was the start of a beautiful relationship with those guys.

They had no idea who just popped into their lives. I say that in a very humble way because I believed in our talents and the ability to market us. I saw the potential of greatness with these guys. But, they seemed to be happy just playing at the Hilton hotel on the weekends.

The combination of my persistence in marketing us in New York city with the pure talent was a great combination. I needed them to see what I saw. I saw four guys who could capture the music world with original and creative music in a style that was sexy and fun. We were only a few months behind the Harry Connick Jr. craze and we had a great story. A local friend, Henry Vaccaro Jr. was managing singer John Eddie and I tried to get him to manage me. Henry was a marketing genius and I knew that if I had him on my team I could have been huge. Henry passed on me and I was on my own. Henry's father was best buddies with Johnny Cash and I knew that he would have been great for my career. My plan was to do a few showcases and get us in the right venues so that record executives would be able to see us live. I convinced the band to make a six song CD for us to shop. Now all I had to do was sell it. I had no idea what I was doing. That is what made it all exciting.

I would sing at any opportunity. Here I am with Marcus Allen during the NFL player's party at the SuperBowl.

New York City, San Francisco and Tony Bennett

I went to New York City and tried to get some gigs. I met with a whole lot of club owners. One night, I walked into BB Kings and met a pretty girl by the name of Trish Bleier. Trish was working for Tony Bennett and his son Danny Bennett. Trish and I instantly became friends and we turned out to be good friends. I respect Trish and her business savvy ways. She was a winner and I wanted to be with her as much as possible. Her kindness opened a lot of doors for me during this time. Trish understood what I was trying to do and she inspired me.

This was the pinnacle of my singing career being with Tony Bennett

I was raised on Tony Bennett. The name Tony Bennett in my family was like high royalty. My mom still talks about how she took a photo of Tony Bennett walking down the street in New York City back in the late 50's. Bennett was my father's favorite singer. My mother was a Frank Sinatra fan. It was a house divided, although both singers were Italians. Tony has always been one of my favorite singers. My mother and I still get into debates about the two singers.

I love Frank but Tony was cool and raw. That's what made him so incredible. Just listen to a younger Tony Bennett and how he uses phasing to sing. It was like creating a work of art with your voice. Tony also had all the coolest cats playing on his gigs. Not to say that Frank wasn't cool. Frank made cool, cool! Frank was the smoothest crooner of all. Then again, Nat King Cole was smooth, like a red velvet cake. Tony was raw and that was more my style of singing.

Trish started to invite me to all the social events that Tony was attending. That is how I met Carol Burnett, Michael Feinstein and Liza Minelli. Then I met Tony Bennet when he was being roasted at the Friars Club in NYC.

With Liza Minelli, Tony Bennett and Carol Burnett
and Trish Bleier at the Friars Club in New York City

Trish and I were sitting at his table in the center of the room. It felt as if all 400 guests were looking at us like, who the hell were we and why were we sitting with Tony Bennett. I guess if you're sitting with Tony Bennett, you must be someone special. If they only knew that I was saying the same thing. How in the hell did I get there? The room was jammed packed with so much talent. Many famous people who ever worked with or wanted to work with Tony were there.

The Friars Club was only for members of high society in New York City. I had no idea how this kid from Long Branch got there. All I knew was that I had to keep smiling and shake as many hands as possible. After I met Tony Bennett, we became instant friends. He was soft spoken and very kind. Tony had an aura around him that only reinforced his greatness. I never saw him upset or rude. Tony is a complete gentleman and that is why people love him. That is also why he has lasted the test of time.

Tony took an interest in me. He even secretly loaned me a few guys from his band in San Francisco. I recorded a CD with them and his son, Dae Bennett, at Bennet Studios formally known as the Hillside Studios in New Jersey. I was told that Tony made a few calls for me. After securing gigs for my band at the Bitter End, The Metropious, Café, Union Station, The Supper Club and BB Kings in New York City, I can only assume it was because of him. It was never confirmed that he did, but how else could I have gotten the largest jazz venues in New York City? They all suddenly wanted Mike Attardi and his big band?

That was one of the most exciting times in my life. I was singing at the Supper Club and singing at BB Kings. Those gigs set the bar for me. It was never surpassed, until my concert with Tess Marsalis and her big band, which was back in my hometown of Long Branch.

I'll never forget being back stage with my band at the Bitter End Club in New York City. My stomach was turning in fear. I never get like that. I was a field goal kicker who played at the professional level. I never felt that much fear in my life up to that point. Someone had told me that Tony Bennett and Dr. John were in the audience. I peeked out from behind the curtain and there they were sitting in the back. I looked at my guys as if I was going to get sick. I kept on blaming the Chinese food I had earlier, but that wasn't the case. It was nerves and I never knew how fear felt until that moment. I guess I wasn't as confident as I used to be kicking a football in front of seventy-thousand fans.

Chico asked if I was okay, while Gladstone was handing me a drink of water. I was spilling the water all over me as if I had a hole in my lips and couldn't get the water into my mouth. I looked at Vinnie and said. "Are they going to like me? Am I good enough? Are they going to like me?" Without skipping a beat Vinnie says. "You have got to make them like you man. Go out there and make them love you." I replied, "That's your words of wisdom?" Then, the little bit of water I managed to get down came right back up with a vengeance. Chico started to laugh.

What he said was like a light bulb that went on. I could finally see the light. That night we received three standing ovations. We were also approached by Eddie Eckstein of Mercury Records. Eddie wanted to set up a showcase for Mercury Records executives to hear us in a month.

The next day I started to write with Jay Brower, who was the Big Band arranger for the famous singer Jerry Vale. We prepared four songs for our band's showcase in New York City. I spent a few weeks with Jay near Meir Woods in California. We wrote some incredible music together. I returned from San Francisco and went to work on the new songs with my band. It was some magical and creative two weeks of making music. I grew as a musician and singer on that trip to San Francisco.

My band saw something in me that they never saw before. I had super confidence after that experience with Jay. The same confidence I had when I walked on a football field to make a field goal. That was missing with my music, until I took that trip to California. I guess you can say that I found my "Mojo in San Francisco!" That was the last time I had ever had the honor to work with Jay Brower. We had a magical collaboration going on, but then life seems to take you down paths you never thought you would travel.

A Defining Moment in Music that Led Me to Love

With the Uptown Horns at the Metropolis Café in NYC 1994

On March 10th, 1994, our band with the Uptown Horns, showed up for our showcase. Eddie Eckstein of Mercury Records, wanted to see my Big Band at a private showcase in New York City. The Uptown Horns were from Saturday Night and they came in to play for us. A friend of mine knew these cats and they came in a learned our original arrangements in an hour. That four- piece horn section was incredible. These guys were real professionals who loved playing swing music. We killed it!

With the rise of popular Big Band music and Harry Connick Jr., Eddie thought my style and original music would also be a hit. We were flawless with our first three songs and saw the excitement in their eyes. After the third song, I paused. It was like all time had stopped for a moment. I looked at the four guys from the Uptown Horns and smiled. They all smiled back as if they knew I was about to get a contract.

I looked at Chico, Gladstone and Vinnie and said, "Men, thank you! This is the end of the road for me." Chico and Gladstone looked at me in disbelief. Vinnie smiled and said "I dig you man. Go out on your terms. I respect that" I smiled back to Vinnie.

I was in a daze as Eddie was about to hand me our contract. I turned it down. I looked at Eddie and said, "I want to be on your side, making the calls and not having to sing for my supper." Eddie looked at me and smiled. That was it. I wanted so much more out of life and this road of singing had come to an end. That was one of the hardest decisions I ever had to make, but at the time I thought it was the best move for me. I was tired of having people be in control of my destiny. I was also growing weary of people telling me what to do and how to do it. I was also very young with a lot of dreams and aspirations of being a star. I had to do this for me and the whole time I realized that I was doing it for the band.

I loved singing but I wasn't finished with the NFL yet. I felt if I was to start singing and going on tour with my band, I was never going to pursue my dream to kick in the NFL again. When Trish heard that I turned down the Mercury Records deal, she was very upset. It was never said, but I think Tony had a lot to do with me getting that showcase. We never talked about it ever again.

After my showcase, I headed back to New Jersey for a short time. While I was there, I took the Kaplan Law Review Course and then took my LSAT in May 1993. I scored a 44 and was accepted into the University of Montana Law School on a full-ride offer. I knew I would be heading to Montana very soon. I also knew that I wanted to start training for football as well.

A few months before I was to head to Montana, my buddy Henry Vacarro Jr., talked me into going to a local nightclub with him. He owned the nightclub BLONDIES. When I walked in, I saw all my friends. I also met a beautiful girl, Monica Cole-Hatchard, who would later turn out to be my future sister-in-law, Monica Nordell.

One-day Monica asked me over to meet her parents, Richard and Sandra Cole-Hatchard. We had a wonderful time with lots of laughs. Monica then introduced me to her beautiful, younger sister. Her name was Colleen. She was sitting in her room and we popped our heads in to say hello. She was one of the most beautiful girls I ever had seen. I felt from the moment I met her that there was chemistry between us. I was right, we developed a wonderful friendship. Several years later Colleen became my wife. She always said that the only thing she remembers about the first time we met was that "The guy wears too much aftershave."

I invited Monica and Colleen to come see me in a show at the Spring Lake Theater later that summer. I told her that I would be doing a new musical by Sondheim. I performed as Cinderella's Prince in Steven Sondheim's new musical called Into the Woods. Monica and Colleen did show and we had a great time. We all had a wonderful conversation after the show and I realized that Colleen and I had a lot in common. Monica had to go to some party and suggested that Colleen and I hang out that night. I wanted to get to know her and I thought she felt the same way about me.

In our conversation, I told her that I would be leaving very soon to go to the University of Montana's Law School. I could see by her reaction that she was happy for me, but she also appeared to be a little sad that I would be leaving so soon. She played hard to get and I think that is why I fell in love with her. Time flew by so fast that summer when I was with Colleen. Before I knew it, it was almost time to leave for University of Montana's Law School.

My Wife Colleen on the left and my sister in law Monica.

A few days before I was going to leave, I planned to have a surprise concert for my acting teacher, Mr. Vincent Borelli. Tess Marsalis and I were going to perform the concert. It was to raise money for Mr. Borelli's theatre program at Long Branch High School. Tess Marsalis was the former wife to the famous jazz musician Branford Marsalis.

Tess was like Billie Holiday. Her voice was beautiful and honest. She sang with conviction and respect for jazz. I learned so much from Tess who naturally was a great singer. Tess made singing effortless and smooth. It was almost like singing with a veteran singer who was crafting her art for years. I first heard Tess sing in Shrewsbury, New Jersey at the Monmouth County library. She was with her eighteen- piece big band and it was amazing. Her show inspired me to find local guys to put together a big band. Several days later, we had a big band.

I wanted to have the concert in the old theater of the old school, but local school politics were keeping us out. My friend, Joseph Ferraina, knew that performing the concert meant a lot to me. He knew I felt it was important for me to give back to the school, my teacher and friend, Vincent Borelli. If it wasn't for Joseph that concert would have never happened. Joseph still to this day is a great friend and mentor.

Tess and I sang several duets that night to rave critic reviews. The concert was Michael Attardi and his Big Band's last gig. That was the last time I sang as a professional. I went out on top singing with my friend Tess and my band.

The Battle of My Life Again

I went to law school for two weeks and then flew back home. Not only was I homesick, but Colleen, who would become the love of my life was in New Jersey, not Montana. When I got back to New Jersey, I went to Westwood Manor.

I moved back to the home I grew up in. A few days later, Colleen and I went to Action Park, a water theme park in North Jersey. I remember that we just wanted to get away and have some fun. We were having such a great day until I came home and Colleen noticed that I had red blotches all over my body.

Immediately, we went to the hospital and they admitted me on the spot. My doctors had no idea at first what was going on with me. Then they took a blood test and learned that I had a severe low count of platelets. Platelets are needed to heal your body. My platelets were being killed off and no one knew why. My mother, Colleen and grandmother took care of me during my sickness. I continued to battle through and never lost hope.

I went through several blood transfusions. They also tested me for every type of cancer. My body was killing off the platelets as soon as we were putting them back in. My health continued to deteriorate. I lost 50 pounds in a few weeks and was down to 145 pounds.

I was in my hospital room with my family and Colleen. My oncologist was a specialist surgeon. He walked in and said that I needed to get my spleen removed. He thought my spleen was killing off my platelets. He also said that my surgery was very risky. I had a 50% chance of living. My platelets were low. He said that they may not be able to stop me from bleeding to death on the operating table.

The next morning when it was time for the surgery, my family was in the room. We had been in this situation once before and I really didn't want to be there again. I began hearing echoes from the past when I was only 24 years old and had to have my cancer surgery. I thought that was the battle of my life. I didn't think after only a few years, I would be facing another life and death situation at the age of 27. The surgery and recuperation was so difficult the last time. It was a hard road and the thought of going through this all over gain was painful. I felt more fearful this time because of my odds. I had to find the strength to muster up an "I can do it" attitude. I knew I had to be strong if I wanted to survive.

I was under anesthesia as the doctors performed the operation. I was unaware of anything. If someone told me the story that I am about to tell, I would say they were crazy or that they are making a really good story.

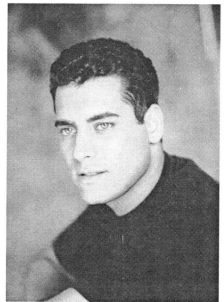

I was 25 here and recovering from the first surgery

I had an out of the body experience. It was so real. I saw myself laying on the operating table. I saw the operating table floating upward to a bright light. As clear as day, I saw my grandparents, aunts and uncles that had all passed on. They all were calling me over, as if I was late for dinner. I remember feeling peaceful and relaxed. I had no pain or worries. I truly cannot explain the joy and pleasure I was experiencing. If this was heaven, I was ready to go. That was the only time I felt safe without any fear. It must have been heaven.

But before I reached the end of the warm bright light, I began to wake up. I found myself staring at the bright hospital lights as I was coming out of my daze. I saw the doctors working tirelessly to revive me. The doctor stood over me and said, "Good to have you back Michael, you're a fighter."

After the surgery, I went to the recovery room and then to my hospital room. When I woke up, Colleen and my family were there. I knew when I looked at Colleen that I was going to marry her. She had stood by me during the most horrific time in my life. Maybe, I did die and she was my assigned angel sent by God to protect me. She still protects me every day. Either way, God gave her to me and I cherish our life together. Did I just beat death once again?

Colleen slept at the hospital every night while I was there. She would hold my hand and tell me that I was going to get better and stronger. To this day, she teases me about when I was confessing my love to her. As she tells the story, I was holding my pain pump in my left hand. As soon as I administrated the morphine in my system to stop the pain, I would look up at her. My eyes felt like they were rolling back in my head as I said, "I love you so much." Then I looked at my pump. I'd franticly began pushing the button several times until she released my thumb off the pump. I said, "Is this thing working? Is this pump thing working?" She calmly said, "Yes, it's working." She is a remarkable and smart human being, who always sees the good in people. I would never be the man I am today if not for my incredible wife Colleen.

This was a serious moment in my life and I needed to get over my health issues once and for all. I started to change the way I ate and how I exercised. It was a second wake-up call for me. I knew what I needed to do and what it would take to have a better life.

A New Day-A New Venture

The healing and rehabilitation process was long. Finally, I was strong enough and healthy enough to go back home. Being in the hospital for so long sparked an idea. I was going to start my own high school sports paper. This paper would give back to my community.

I went to see my great friend, Joseph Ferraina. He was the superintendent of schools at Long Branch and I told him my idea. Joe loaned me $1,000.00 to start up the paper and I paid him back a month later. If it wasn't for Joe Ferraina, I would not have had a paper. I thank him all the time!

When I started my paper, I had no idea how I was going to do it. I knew that I loved sports and wanted to help kids and give back to my community. I was determined to turn a negative into a positive. I went around to my friends who had businesses and started my first issue on April 1, 1996. I struggled at first, but then a big break came with one of the largest car dealers on the Jersey Shore. The owner's name was Joe Sansone and he was the GM for Sansone Auto in Neptune, New Jersey.

Joe was a happy guy who was well respected. I went to see Joe to ask for advertising. I waited for days to see him. I showed up every day for a whole week trying to get a meeting. Joe was so busy making deals that I never got a chance to see him until the Monday of the following week. As Joe walked out of his office with a client, I overheard them talking about the New York Giant's game. They were discussing how their kicker missed a 37-yard field goal. I jumped up and said, "I can make a 37 yarder all day long". They both laughed. "I can! In fact, I will show you."

Joe was intrigued. We went outside and I ran to my car and pulled out a football. I asked two salesmen to stand ten yards apart. I turned to Joe and said, "If I make this kick, you will have to take a full-page ad in my paper." Joe replied, "If you miss, I get the ad for free." We shook hands and agreed.

Joe took the ball and moved it back 15 yards. Joe turned to his client and said. "If this kid makes this 50-yard field goal, you pay the number I gave you on the truck. If he misses, you get your number." Both Joe and his client agreed. Joe held the ball and I kicked it. The ball went straight between the two salesmen and hit a new parked car on the hood. A little dent but Joe didn't care. It was all about the rush it gave us all at that moment.

The kick would have been good from 60 yards. Joe turned and smiled, "You got my ad!" That was a start of a great relationship and friendship. I was heartbroken to learn that he passed from a massive heart attack a few years later.

That story is still told today and some think it's an urban legend. It's not, it really happened. I got the idea from another car dealer by the name of Kenny Schwartz. He passed a football 70 yards to get a guy to sell him his first used cars. We both still laugh about how crazy we were and what would've happened if we didn't win the bet.

I'd be giving a free full- page ad in my paper and it would have put me right out of business. When I walked into Sansone's Auto, I knew I was going to get an ad, I didn't know how or when. Joe was a great businessman. Either way, he had nothing to lose. I worked hard for several months to build up that paper. It was a labor of love and I wanted it to be a success. I started to save money and life was getting better for Colleen and me.

With the very first money that Colleen and I started to make, we could travel. We loved to travel. We have traveled the world and had some incredible experiences. We've been to Germany, Austria, Switzerland, England, France, Spain, Italy, Wales, Sweden, Norway, Japan, Vietnam, Mexico, Bermuda, Bahamas, Granada, Dominican Republic, Saint Maarten, Haiti, Grand Cayman Islands, Puerto Rico and 34 states including Maui, Kauai and the big island of Hawaii.

With every travel adventure, there comes a story. There are so many stories, that I could write four books about them all.

I still had a dream to make films. I started to write more and compose music. I was using some of the paper money to create more content for my film ideas. Several months later, I met Dominic Ambrosio who worked for HBO. Dominic and I met because a car dealer owed me money and was using Dominic as a bargaining chip. If I was to take half of what the car dealer owed me, he would, in return, introduce me to Dominic from HBO. I had nothing to lose since half was better than nothing. If Dominic was real, then maybe it wasn't such a bad deal after all.

I called Dominic at HBO. "Hello, I'm trying to reach Dominic Ambrosio." "I'm Dominic, whose calling?" I replied, "This is Mike Attardi and the car dealer who sold you your car asked me to call you for a meeting." Dom replied, "That bum sold me a lemon. I want my money back, you tell him. He's got the nerve to have you call me? What do you want?" I replied, "I wanted to meet you. I can see that he's playing a game with us now. He sold you a lemon and he owes me money. This is not a good time, is it? Dominic started to laugh and said, "He owes you money and avoids all my calls. He sold me a crappy car and he connects us?"

We both started to laugh. Dom says, "What are you doing tomorrow? Come into the city and let's get lunch. We may not have come over on the same ship, but we're in the same boat." That was the start a wonderful relationship. Dominic was a huge influence in my journey towards film making. He is still one of my most trusted friends and an all-around great human being to the world.

The Comeback Kid- Bill Parcells

I was getting stronger by the day. I knew it was time for me to start training again. I gave it my all. At that time, my friend, worked for the U.S. Postal Service. He told me that Coach Bill Parcells was living in Sea Girt, New Jersey. That was only 30 minutes away from me.

I had heard that Coach Parcells was a spiritual man who liked underdogs. I wrote him a heartfelt letter, drove to his house in Sea Girt, New Jersey and slipped it through the mail slot in his door. I was never so stupid, but I had nothing to lose. I ran up to his door and ran back to my car as if I just made a bookie drop. At one point, I almost went back to retrieve it. That would have been great if I'd gotten caught.

Two weeks passed with no word. Then one day our home telephone rang and Colleen answered it and handed me the phone. She said, "there's someone on the phone from the New York Jets?" I asked, "Is it Coach Parcells?" Colleen replied, "How would I know? I don't know what Coach Parcells sounds like," she handed me the phone.

At first, I thought it was one of my friends pranking me. Then I realized that I never told anyone about the letter. After she handed me the phone, she realized who it was and smiled at me. Coach Parcells said, "You know I have to bring you up to Hofstra University now. You had the nerve to come to my house, slip his letter through my mail slot of my front door in broad daylight. Anyone who does that deserves a tryout. Besides, my wife read the letter and told me I had to give you a tryout." I laughed.

He went on to say, "I knew you were with the Raiders. I'll see you in a few days. I'll have a member of my staff arrange all the logistics." Then the he hung up the phone. In disbelief, Colleen hugged me knowing that this could be my last chance to kick in the NFL.

A few days later, I was at Hofstra University at the New York Jets training facility. I was getting ready to kick for legendary Coach Bill

Parcells. I was out on the practice field for over 45 minutes. We started kicking from the extra points up to the 60 yard-line. I only missed one out of forty kicks. The right hash-mark on the 48 yard-line.

Kickers seem to know all their missed kicks. As I had looked around, I had never seen Coach Parcells. Then out of nowhere, he appeared behind me. "Son, that was the best kicking display I've seen in years. What am I going to do with you, Attardi? I have another year contract with John Hall. Now you're coming back into the game after a battle with cancer and no spleen. I can't keep two kickers. You mark my word, if anything happens to John Hall this season, you will be my first call." I thanked Coach for the opportunity and shook his hand.

Coach Parcells made a bunch of points with God that day. Coach was kind and generous to give me that opportunity to kick one more time for the NFL. I will never forget what he did for me as a player but most of all, as a man. I only met him for that short time. But, he will always be in my heart for giving me a chance to say that I gave it my all, one last time. I retired from football on top. Kicking for legend Coach Bill Parcells. My NFL Career was officially over, but I was at total peace with that.

As I was driving home from Hofstra, New York, I had the realization that life is what you make of it. I turned on the radio and God as my witness, Frank Sinatra was singing "My Way." I rolled down my car window and start singing with Frank as loud as I could.

Regrets, I've had a few
But then again, too few to mention
I did what I had to do
And saw it through without exemption

I planned each charted course
Each careful step along the byway
And more, much more than this
I did it my way

Yes, there were times, I'm sure you knew when
I bit off more than I could chew
But through it all, when there was doubt
I ate it up and spit it out
I faced it all and I stood tall

And did it my way

The guy in the car next to me must have thought I was nuts. I didn't care, it was my moment with Frank and only he knew how I felt at that time. I drove in front of that guy moments later and paid his New Jersey Turnpike toll. He caught up to me and thanked me for the nice gesture. I said, "No worries pal. I did it my way! He smiled and I drove off singing.

My Bachelor Party- Casa de Campo

Scott Seeley, Me, Tom Guilford, Jim Dowd and Doug Dunn at Casa DeCampo

In 1998. I was at the NFL Alumni Golf Tournament in Montclair, New Jersey. They were holding a super-raffle for $100 a chance and I won a trip to Casa de Campo in the Dominican Republic. This was a great opportunity for me to get my friends together for one week to play golf before I got married. We planned my bachelor party trip in April 1999. All my best friends were not able to attend so we had another bachelor golf party a few weeks later in New Jersey.

My friends, Doug Dunn, Scott Seeley, Tom Gilford and Jim Dowd all flew down to this incredible resort. We were in the lobby of the hotel and Doug recognized the famous actor George Hamilton. He had just checked-in. We had a few cocktails with George before going to our hacienda. George was friendly and polite, a true gentleman.

It was like paradise. The four-bedroom condo on the golf course called the Teeth of the Dog. It had open face bunkers with railroad ties, and the only way out of them, was backwards. That was a common and famous design by Pete Dye.

This paradise hacienda had three floors. There were three bedrooms on the bottom floor. On the second floor, there was a kitchen and a living room. On the third floor, there was one single loft bedroom. I stayed in my own room on the third floor. It turned out to be a smart move. Most of the guys wanted to party all night long. I was all about getting a good night's rest and playing golf for the next five days. This was a Pete Dye golf course. I was excited at the thought of playing at this famous golf course.

The resort staff gave me and the guys several warnings when we checked in. They told us not to venture into the city. It would be too dangerous. The guys decided to go to the city of Punta Cana anyway. The guys got so drunk that at 4 AM I heard loud noises coming from the front of our condo. When I went outside, I saw my friend Doug in his underwear, holding an 8-iron golf club in his hands. He was waving it back-and-forth at three guys that were holding large machetes.

I tried to be calm as I asked them, "What the hell was going on?" One of the guys holding a machete said: "This guy stole my golf cart." I looked at Doug and asked him if he had stolen his golf cart? With a drunken smile, he started to laugh and said: "Yes, we needed a ride back."

I turned to the guy with machete and asked, "How much would it cost for me to rent the golf cart?" They huddled together and turned around and said $50. So, I pulled out my wallet, gave them $100 and told them to go away and to allow us to have it for the next two days and they agreed. We had a lot of fun with that golf cart. I never knew that you could do a pop a wheelie and jump over things in a golf cart.

The fifth hole on Teeth of the Dog Golf Course at Casa De Campo

The next morning, I woke up early to try to get the guys out to play golf. Unfortunately, only Scott Seeley dragged himself out of the bed to play. The Teeth of the Dog was an unbelievable golf course with a lot of water hazards, especially on the ocean side. At hole number 5, the green is on an island surrounded by sand bunkers and located right on the ocean. It was 137 yards to the pin. We had a slight wind in our faces so I decided to use a strong 8-iron. I struck the ball solid. At first, I thought I hit it over the green. The ball was heading right towards the pin and then we both lost it in the shadows. Then from the connecting golf hole next to us, a guy runs over and starts shouting, "Holy Shit! Holy Shit!"

Out of nowhere, actor George Hamilton and his friend ran over to our green. Scott and I did not know what was going on, so we got in our golf cart to drive down to see. When we got to the green, Hamilton said, "Who in the hell made that shot? I can't believe it, I've never seen a ball fly right into the hole like that." Scott and I ran over to the hole and there it was, a huge divot taken out the backside of the cup and my ball lying there. My golf ball flew right in the hole and stuck the back of the cup. George walked over to me and put his arm around me and said, "Drinks are on you my boy, I'll see you back at the hotel bar." Still in disbelief, I picked up my Titleist 2 ball and we went off to play the rest of the round. I was excited to have drinks with George. But more exciting that I just made a hole in one.

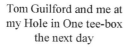
Tom Guilford and me at my Hole in One tee-box the next day

When we got back to the resort bar it was like a scene from Animal House. There were 200 people there. George Hamilton had told everyone about my hole-in-one. They were all waiting to see us. I went to the bar and George walked up to me. He put his arm around me and said to the crowd who became silent, "Hey everyone, this is him, this is my friend." He then turned to me and said, "What's your name?" I said, "Michael." He turned back to the crowd and said, "This is my friend Michael, he made a hole-in-one today and drinks are on him."

The crowd had been silent when George talked. Now from the once silent crowd came the biggest roar I've ever heard. I could swear there were also sounds of bass pounding with techno music following. All my friends surrounded me and people started to order drinks. Never in my life was I so scared about receiving a bar bill. The people were drinking bottles of Dom Perignon, Johnny Walker Blue and other expensive drinks. When the celebration was over, the bartender handed me the bill for $3,789. I was about to chuck-up my lunch from earlier that day. I remember thinking, I'm not even married and Colleen is going to divorce me because that was our wedding money.

I remember Doug turning to me and saying, "I'll give you a couple hundred dollars towards it." A couple hundred dollars was like putting a Band-Aid on an axe wound at that point. George came over and put his arm around me and said, "that was the greatest golf shot I've ever seen live." He picks up the check from my shaking hands and said, "this one's on me, let's call it an early wedding present." All my friends started to laugh, knowing that George was picking up the bill. All I remember hearing was the kick of techno base music pounding and me jumping in the air with joy. I took the Dom Perignon bottle. Then drank what was left like a gangster rap star.

George was a great guy. We had a lot of fun with him and I'll never forget that experience. Years later, my sister Francine met him at Monmouth Park racetrack and told George that she was my sister. He smiled and said, "That was the greatest golf shot I ever saw. The ball flew right into the hole. But what was more entertaining was seeing your brother's face when he handed that bar bill!" Thank you, George!" He will leave a legacy.

Golf is in my DNA. I love playing this game with family and friends

An Olympic Gold Story- USA vs. Russia

My mother loved skating. She always watched the Winter Olympics. She loved to follow ice dancing and figure skating. She would take us out on Franklin Lake in West Long Branch, New Jersey, whenever the lake was frozen over. Don't forget, the Jersey Shore is cold in the winter. I would play a pick-up game of hockey while my sisters would pretend that they were Peggy Fleming. I know if we had lived in Canada, my mom would have wanted me to be a hockey player and my sisters, figure skaters.

I was raised during the "Cold War" and the Reagan years and anything Russian was considered bad. That is how we were taught in school. Who could forget the 1980 "Miracle on Ice" when the United States beat Russia in hockey? The Olympics became the United States versus Russia games. I remember watching the 1994 Winter Olympics ice dancing with my family. I was watching this Russian couple go up against a United States couple. I remember routing for the Russian's to fail. My mother was the opposite, she was all about the art and beauty of skating and not about the politics.

The Russians did win Gold and I understood what my mother was saying about skating. Their skating program was flawless and smooth. I have never seen a better program then watching the Olympic Ice Dancing in my life. No matter what sport it is, if it's mastered at the highest level, everyone will enjoy the competition.

However, I do know that most former NFL players wouldn't go out to a bar and ask the bartender to turn his television channel to ice dancing. You should have seen all the looks I received one night when I was with my mother and I did ask. It was different because my mother was with me and we were sharing a sporting moment together.

When the couple finished with their program, my mother had the biggest smile. The same one when I did something amazing and she approved. The Russian ice skaters were Evgeny Platov and Oksana Grishuk. I liked these skaters because of their talent. I also liked them because they gave a humble interview after they learned the Gold medal was theirs. I remember Evgeny thanking his parents and all the people who got him to the Olympics. I saw him as a great athlete, not a Russian, which we were all taught in high school to be an enemy. In so many ways, I saw myself in him.

Evgeny Platov is a Russian former competitive ice dancer. He is best known for his partnership with Oksana Grishuk from 1989 through 1998. While he was with Grishuk, he was a two-time Gold Medal Olympic Champion in 1994 and 1998. He was also a four-time World Champion from 1994-1997, a three-time European Champion from 1996-1998 and a four-time World Champion from 1994-1997.

Colleen and I with our friends Maya Usova and Evgeny Platov

In 1999, I was working on my sports publication and stopped by to visit an advertiser at the Wall Ice Arena. This was the only hockey area in our area and every high school would train and play hockey there. I was there to meet with the General Manager in his office to go over some advertising options. I looked out his window that overlooked the whole area inside.

I saw this couple skating and was so mesmerized by their timing and pure talent that I asked who they were. Immediately he said, Evgeny Platov and Maya Usova from Russia. At first, I could not believe my own ears. I said, "You're telling me, the Olympic Gold Medal Champion, Evgeny Platov is right there skating?" He replied, "Yes, he moved to Marlboro, New Jersey and he is training here with his new partner and Russian coach." I immediately became obsessed with wanting to meet him and do a story in our sports paper about him.

I was introduced to him after their practice. He put out his hand and said, "Evgeny." I responded, "Who are you calling a Ginney? I'm an Italian and now you're calling me a Ginney. That's disrespectful." Evgeny was in shock! I shook his hand and said, "I'm only kidding around comrade." He smiled at me and ever since that day, we have been best friends. Evgeny was at my wedding in 1999, and was one of my first friends to hold my first born, Michael Jr. in the hospital in 2003. He was the first of my friends to hold our second son, Nathaniel in 2006. We have had so many journeys and laughs together and we also love to play golf.

Evgeny is one of my most trusted and closest friends. He has introduced me to his world of skating and I have introduced him to the NFL and movie making. To this day, I call him Alligator and he calls me Tomato. My favorite claim to fame with Evgeny was when we were playing a game in an arcade. I beat him four times in the USA verses Russia's table top hockey game. I won twice with the USA team and twice as the Russian team. I just count it as a tie to make him feel better. By the way, I'm still waiting for him to try and beat me in a round of golf!

It's All in the Cards

My great friends Larry Little and Phil Villapiano

I wanted to ask Colleen to marry me, but it was too soon because I wanted to have our own home to move into first. I wanted the best for her. I knew I needed more money to buy a house. So, instead of asking Colleen to marry me right away, we stayed at Westwood Manor to save our money. Even though we were paying rent to my grandmother, we were still able to save a few dollars, but it wasn't enough. Then one day, a friend called me. He knew I had purchased baseball and football cards since I was 10 years old. He also knew I had an amazing card collection.

He told me about this sports card auction where this guy from New York City goes and spends big money. He was always in the market for older 1950s- thru 1970s sports cards. I decided to turn the hobby that I loved into a way to raise money. I didn't know what I had until I started to take all my cards out to research them. My cards were worth big money and I had to find a way to get in front of this guy from New York.

I went to VFW in Port Monmouth, bought a table and set up all my cards to sell. The guy from New York City arrived on a ferry boat and walked around the auction. You could see the other dealers foaming at the mouth waiting for him to look at their cards. Fights would breakout. Some of the dealers would push their way into sales at other booths. Not even ethical for New Jersey standards.

My friend told the guy that I was a former NFL player and that I had some incredible cards for sale. The guy seemed more excited to meet me because I was a former NFL player than to buy any of my cards. The guy asked, "So what was it like playing with Howie Long and Marcus Allen?" I replied, "It was one of the most exciting times in my life to be able to play with future Hall of Fame players like those two. Not only that, I had Art Shell as a head coach and Al Davis as an owner. How much better does it get?" He shook his head and agreed and said, "How long have you've been collecting cards?" I replied, "Since I was 10. I used to go to the Sheraton Hotel sports card show in Freehold, New Jersey and buy my cards there. I met Mickey, Duke, Willie and Hank there." I didn't have to use last names with those great Hall of Fame players. The guy knew exactly who I was talking about.

The guy was pulling out hundred-dollar bills. When he opened my card booth glass top table his eyes lit up. "Is that a 1961 Mantle and Maris in mint condition?" I nodded yes and handed them to him. "I've been looking all over for several years for these."

Without hesitation, he offers me $1,000.00 for the pair. I countered and said $1,400.00. He came back and said $1,200 and not a penny more. I shook his hand. We both knew that this was going to be a great relationship. Every dealer at that show was looking at me as if I stole something. I did! Their business away from this guy from New York.

He gave me his card and asked to meet me outside of the auction. I agreed and met him. He bought part of my sports card collection for $25,000.00. I still have a great collection left. But I always knew that someday the card collection business was going to end. I needed to unload some of my content too. So, I all sold all my comic books and made an extra $5,000. I took that money and bought silver and stored it away for a rainy day. My thought was, if all went to the crapper, you will always be able to sell or trade silver. I started to build up a coin collection and stored it away in a bank safe deposit box.

Two years later, sports cards took a huge hit and most cards lost most of their values. You may be asking, what did I do with the $25,000.00? I invested that money into stocks of four little, unknown companies. One was Cisco Systems, Sun Micro Systems, Nokia and Lucent Technology.

We turned that $25,000.00 into $90,000.00 in less than two years. We found our first home in Port Monmouth and we used that money to buy our first house. We also took a three-week vacation to Hawaii that year.

I was sitting on Waikiki Beach with Colleen, sipping my Scotch on the Rocks. I began looking at the beautiful waves crashing on the shore. I remember turning to Colleen and saying, "Not bad for my baseball and football picture cards that were on cardboard." We both toasted with our drinks and I smirked at her knowing that she got a kick out of my corny sense of humor.

My father in law, Richard
and I sailing in Hawaii.

My Wife is Wonder Woman

Our Wedding Day June 1990

My sports paper was growing and I had made money from my collections. I was getting back on solid financial ground again. So, I decided it was now time to ask Colleen to marry me.

Colleen and I had been thinking about buying a house in West Long Branch. But we got into a bidding war and decided not to pursue the bidding. Colleen was very sad about the news. I wanted to cheer her up so I took her out for her favorite sandwich. When we got to the place that made this sandwich, we read a sign on the door that said, "Out of Business." We were shocked and sad that it had closed.

I decided to take her to buy her favorite ice cream called Coffee Royal next door at Welsh Farms. Colleen waited outside while I ran in to get her ice cream. I looked for the ice cream and couldn't find it. The owner told me that Welsh Farms discontinued making that flavor. I didn't have it in me to tell her at that moment.

Then I asked if she wanted to go out for sushi. Before we went out to eat, I decided to take a drive by the ocean and walk on the boardwalk. I had her engagement ring in my pocket the whole day. It was like burning a hole in my pants. We had a lot of disappointments that day. All I had wanted was for it to be a very special day. We drove to the boardwalk and the minute we got out of my car, it started to rain buckets. We ran back to the car and that's when we both decided to cut our losses and just go out for dinner.

When we arrived at the Sushi place, it was so crowded that we decided to get take-out. On the way home, we stopped at Blockbusters to rent a movie. We ended up bringing home the movie, "Michael" starring John Travolta. It was the movie about John being Saint Michael, the Archangel who comes down from heaven to have a little fun.

When we got back to the house, I was so nervous that I was complaining that the heat was not working. We had no heat and it was the middle of November in New Jersey. Cold for anyone's standards. We stopped the movie for a bathroom break and I ran inside the kitchen. I found an old fortune cookie and placed a small piece of paper inside it. When we were about to turn the movie back on, I offered her a fortune cookie.

I opened mine and said my famous fortune cookie line, "Never play golf in the rain because you'll get your balls wet." That still gets a laugh today. Colleen opened her cookie and started to read her fortune. "You will have an amazing life. Will you marry me?" Then I got down on one knee and held out her ring. She said, "Yes."

We ran upstairs to my parents to tell them the great news then rushed downstairs to tell my grandmother. Everyone in the house was so excited. Colleen and I got in my car to go tell her parents, Richard and Sandra. That was one of the happiest days of my life. Everything we encountered didn't seem to matter anymore. We had lost a house bid, the sandwich restaurant went out of business, our favorite ice cream was discontinued and it rained on us. Fortune cookies don't come with sushi. I guess, it was meant to happen that way.

Music and a Disney Legend

Dani Donadi and I won 96 Awards on the Film Festival Circuit

After we were married, Colleen and I used to take trips to Disney World. We loved going to Epcot. One day while at Epcot, we were walking through Italy and a band called Nova Era was playing. Colleen and I were so moved and excited about their original music because it was so unique and fun. I knew I had to meet them. We waited until they finished their set and then introduced ourselves.

We met Andre Roca who was the leader of the band. I told him that I was interested in working with him. He said he thought that Dani Donadi, a musical composer, would be a better match for me. A few days later he introduced Dani to me. Our meeting went very well. I was impressed by Dani's musical compositions. Dani also liked my work so much that we decided to collaborate on my new original content. My original concept was to create the music for a musical theater show. A few weeks later we began to start writing music together.

Colleen and I got on a flight to fly back to New Jersey. I knew the minute we got back that I had to begin raising money for the upcoming projects that Dani and I would be doing. I began working on securing funds for our project. I was also traveling to Orlando every month. I was connecting with Disney artists and Dani to work on new soundtracks. During this time, I became inspired to create new original content. We wanted to focus on family related projects.

In the year 2000, I flew down to Orlando seven months in a row. I was thrilled to be working with Dani Donati on new musical soundtracks. I felt honored to be with other Disney artists on conceptual animated artwork. On one occasion when I flew back home, my plane had just landed in the New Jersey airport. The minute I landed, I received a call from my friend, Gentry Akens. He told me that the legendary Disney artist, Marc Davis was in Orlando. He said that Marc was going to be signing autographs at a Disney art store in the MGM Hollywood Studios.

I called my wife from the airport and said, "I'm going back to Disney World on the next flight!" She thought I was crazy, but she always supports my spontaneous actions. I never forgot Marc Davis. I knew I had to see him again. I wondered if he would remember meeting me when I was eight years old. Not in a million years!

I arrived at the Art of Animation building at the old MGM Disney Studios. Only one other fan got there before me. The line grew longer with a sea of people wanting to meet the legendary Disney artist. As the doors opened, I experienced the feeling of time moving in slow motion. There Marc was, sitting behind a table. Time had not been a friend to Marc, as he was looking very frail. When it was my turn, his assistant asked me my name.

I was now standing in front of Marc. I unrolled the original artwork he made for me thirty years ago. I did not stammer, when I said, "You're not going to remember this. But you drew this for me when I was eight years old at the Monmouth Mall in New Jersey. Marc looked at the drawing, then looked back at me, once again at the drawing and then he looked straight into my eyes. Marc replied, "You're the kid with that speech impediment." I was stunned. I felt like time had paused and we both smiled at one another.

Marc continued, "Do you have time? We have a lot of catching up to do. Come back in an hour and let's have lunch together." I was still in disbelief that he knew exactly who I was and remembered me after 30 years. I nodded my head, yes. Later that day, Marc and I had lunch at the Brown Derby on the Disney property. He had snuck in a double Martini with olives. Marc invited me to his home in California, but a few weeks later in 2002, he passed away. It was one of the saddest days of my life, when I found out that Marc had died. A piece of my childhood was taken just as I thought I was getting it back after 30 years.

Darryl Dawkins- "Double D"

With Darryl Dawkins and Colleen at Monmouth Park Racetrack in 1989

In 1998, I met Darryl Dawkin. He's better known as "Chocolate Thunder" to all the Philadelphia 76er's fans. I met him when I was covering the Jersey Shore, basketball league. It was at Saint Rose High School in Belmar, New Jersey. I was taking pictures at the game. I used to position myself right under the basket. I captured some great photos of the basketball players driving up the lane going for a slam-dunk.

One game, Darryl Dawkins gets a pass right in the middle lane. He goes up and slams the hardest dunk I've ever seen a man do. Then he came down and landed right on top of me. As a former football player, I have gotten hit many times, but not like this. In football, we have pads and a helmet to protect us. This hit was different. It was body to body with one large man and one triple large man. We both collided like a steam train hitting a Volkswagen Beatle.

It felt like a steam engine slammed on top of my chest. When he got up from my still body, I felt instant relief from my pain. "Did you get it?" Darryl asked. I replied short of breath, "Did I get what?" He said, "The photo of me slamming." "Of course, I did." I said. He smiled and went back to playing the game he loved.

A few days later, I saw him before the first game. I gave him several photographs of himself playing from the other night. He liked them so much that he invited me out to dinner. Later, we went to a place in Belmar called Evelyn's and we had four lobsters. We ate like kings while we talked about football and basketball. Darryl was excited to talk to me about my experiences playing for the Raiders. He had said that he loved football and always wanted to play.

I knew from some of our previous conversations that he liked gambling and loved horse racing. I owned a racehorse that was running at Monmouth Park in Oceanport, New Jersey. My friend, Bill Hogan, and I purchased the horse for a small fee. But we found out that the up-keep of the horse was five times the amount that we had paid for her. We were losing money even before we raced her.

Our horse was running on a Friday in the fifth race that week. The odds were 28 to 1 because it was her first time running at Monmouth Park. I put a few hundred down to win, place and show. "Double D," that is what I used to call Darryl, made the same bet. Our horse came in second place and we won over $1200 a piece that day.

Bill and I also won a place purse of $8,000 dollars. We figured out that this new won money was enough to cover all our expenses for the horse during the racing season. Bill and I agreed that after that racing season we would sell the horse. We sold the horse for three times the amount we paid for her. The horse went on to win nine races and made its new owner over $200,000 in winnings.

Darryl was a fun-loving guy. We used to play a lot of golf on the Jersey Shore. His father-in-law was the starter down at Lakewood County Golf Course. We played golf there for free. But the drive was over an hour to get there. It wasn't worth it, since most of the course was like a cow pasture.

Darryl and I had many laughs and great times. I also helped him during some bad times in his life. He suffered a lot of pain when he and his second wife were going through a divorce. He also shared with me many stories of growing up as a poor kid and having to fight for everything he ever achieved.

God Bless Darryl. He left a huge Legacy!

Darryl went to Evens High School in Orlando. In a surprise move, he opted to enter the NBA draft right out of high school, instead of attending college. He made his decision to help his grandmother, mother and siblings out of poverty. He figured the faster he could make enough money the sooner his family would be out of poverty. He succeeded. He was the first high school player enter the NBA after his high school graduation.

Darryl played in the NBA from 1975-1989. He had a key role in the Sixers winning the Eastern Conference Championship. It established him as one of Philadelphia's top players. Dawkins was averaging 11.7 points and 7.9 rebounds in 25 minutes per game. He also ranked second in the league in points.

In March 2015 Darryl found out that I was now living in Orlando. He called me and said that he was going to come back home to Orlando to visit his family in the fall. He wanted to get together with me for dinner when he got back. I knew he was coaching a few basketball teams in Pennsylvania. He loved coaching and giving back to the kids. Darryl had a huge heart and cared for all humanity.

My friend, Darryl Dawkins died on August 27, 2015, in Allentown, Pennsylvania, at the age of 58. We never got that chance to go out for dinner. I remember when my wife told me the sad news. My heart dropped. I was very depressed that night. Every time I turned a channel on the television. or used my computer, the news of his death would pop-up.

I lost a good friend that day. I didn't talk much about his death to anyone. I was in shock to think that at the young age of 58, my friend will no longer be around to share a good laugh or meet my sons. He was a great friend and I miss him very much.

Michael Strahan and the Hall of Fame

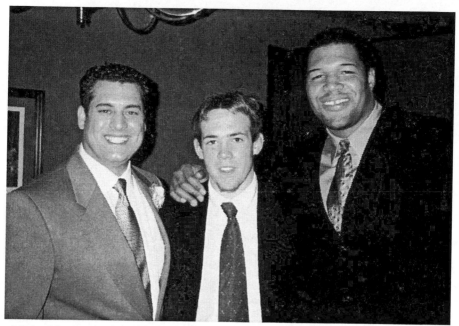

Michael Strahan at my Hall of Fame Induction Night in 2004 with my student kicker Blake

I met Hall of Fame inductee, Michael Strahan, at a football card show in North Jersey. We shared the same football agent and she booked us both for an autograph signing. That was the first year that he was playing for the New York Giants and not a lot of people knew who we were. Everyone thought that there would never be another Lawrence Taylor. How wrong were they?

Michael and I hit it off immediately and later that night we had dinner. You talk about a small world? We found out that the girl he was dating, was the best friend of a girl I was dating. We went out on a few double dates and had some great times. I always knew that Michael was special. He always treated people with respect and was the life of the party. He would listen to what you were saying and Michael never made you feel uncomfortable.

Michael went on to be one of the greatest defense players for the New York Giants, and at that time I was retired from the NFL. We crossed paths several times throughout the years at a few Super Bowl parties. We had always kept in touch, until he got married. After that we didn't have a chance to see each other anymore. His ex-wife never liked me.

He and I spent a lot of time in Atlanta, Georgia, for a while. It was the same year that the Rams won the Super Bowl against the Titians. During that week, I gave him a few tickets to the MVP.com party and I went to the Taste of the NFL instead. What a big mistake!

I was told by many of my friends that went with Michael, that the MVP party was the greatest party of all-time. That night they hung out with Muhammad Ali, Wayne Gretzky, Michael Jordan and John Elway. I saw Michael the next day and he just laughed. "While you were stuffing your face at Taste of the NFL, I was chilling out with Ali, Jordan, Elway and Gretzky. That will teach you to come with me next time. Hey, are you gaining weight Attardi? Taste of the NFL, Huh!"

In 2001, the New York Giants went to the Super Bowl in Tampa and lost to the Baltimore Ravens. I went to that game and saw Michael there. At that time, he was a mega-superstar. But he treated me like the first time we met at that football card show many years earlier. That's how Michael is. He's a great guy with a huge heart.

Michael has gone out of his way to help his friends and even people he's never met. No one ever has anything bad to say about him because he's a quality human being and I'm proud to call him a friend. A friend is someone you don't have to see every day, to know that he's a friend. But when we do see each other, it's like time has never gotten in-between us and we start where we left off.

Right after his Super Bowl loss, I called to cheer him up and talk to him about a few business opportunities. I also shared some special news that I had been elected into my high school Hall of Fame at Long Branch. Never in a million years did I think he would say what he said, "I want to be the person to induct you into your Hall of Fame." I was speechless.

One of the greatest New York Giants of all time, wants to induct me into my high school Hall of Fame. I didn't know what to say. At first, I thought he was joking, but then he asked what time would I need him to be there. I gave him all the details and he drove all the way from North Jersey to be at that event.

I told the Hall of Fame Event Committee that Michael Strahan was coming. Michael inducted me on March 16, 2001. What made this even more special for me, is that it was the day of my grandmother's birthday. That was the greatest gift I could've given my grandmother. She had always stood by me, taught me and helped to make me the man that I am today.

As famous as Michael was, he never treated anybody as if they were beneath him. He's someone who cares more about humanity because he puts others before his own wants or needs. I haven't seen Michael Strahan for several years now. It's not because he's bigger than life. It's not because we are no longer in touch and it's not because we don't have anything in common. He's a mega-star on the national stage and I'm raising three young sons in Florida. I'm sure that if we saw each other tomorrow it would be like not a day has gone by. The one thing that we will always have in common is our incredible friendship.

I respect Michael and I always wish him much success and happiness.

A recent photo of Michael and Me in NYC 2017

Meeting the Grand Master

I wasn't going to give up. I was willing to try anything to have our own family. I looked to my old friend, who knew someone who healed people using Chinese medicine. At the time, my friend and his brother, were studying with a spiritual healer in Los Gatos, California. His name was Grand Master Mac Dom.

My friend Grand Master Mac Dom in California 2002. I was 50 pounds overweight.

The Grand Master was an amazing man who could achieve feats that no other man that I knew could. His story is like a Hollywood movie. Colleen and I talked about me going out to California to see if he could help us. We both agreed that I should go, so I went to California not knowing what was going to happen.

When I arrived, the Grand Master welcomed me at his back door. I stayed there to study the Buddhist way of spiritual living and healing. It was like the movie the Karate Kid. We all had chores to do before the Grand Master would help us with our problems. I stayed with the Grand Master for one month. I saw this man climb up a rope backwards. Then he held his breath under water for over seven minutes. I also saw him doing several two-finger push-ups. That's what I said, two-finger push-ups. When we tried to do it, we almost broke our fingers.

One of the funniest stories I can share with you, is when we were all in the "Sweatbox." That's what we called it. It was a makeshift sauna with cedar benches and walls. It had a little sliding door window and a fire pit. It was a small room with a black boiling cauldron. It was like something out of the movie Harry Potter.

We were all in this hot box together like crowded sardines in a can. We were sweating out the impurities that the Grand Master said we all had within us. At one point, I remember the oxygen level was getting so low that one of my friends got down on all fours to the floor. He was sucking the fresh air from the crack underneath the door. It had to be one of the funniest things I've ever seen, but it was about his survival at that point. The sweat was pouring out of us like we had just ran a twenty-mile marathon with no water breaks.

We will always swear that we saw many different colors of blue, red, and yellow sweat coming out of our bodies. One of my friends said, "I can't breathe the air. It's too thick." I climbed down to the bottom of the floor. I replied, "Come down here. The air is cooler. You can breathe down here." All three of them climbed down towards me. One of my friends said, "What the hell, Attardi, how did you know?" I said, "I didn't miss science class that day. Heat rises as cool air drops." He replies, "Thank you Professor Einstein!"

While we were sweating, we watched the Grand Master Mac Dom open a little window from above. Then he threw several crystals into the black cauldron. Grandmaster, with broken English, said to everyone, "How are you doing?" We all replied, "Just Great!" The temperature in our room that was once over 120° turned ice cold. Now we were shivering like someone had thrown us into an ice-cold lake in Alaska without any clothes.

One of my friends said, "I'm freezing! What the hell did he put in that boiling pot?" Two of my other pals, jumped up to the top seating area and one of them said, "I'm coming up here because heat rises. Right, Attardi?" We were freezing for about 15 minutes. Then the Grand Master opened that little window again. Grandmaster said, "First you hot and now you cold." He gave a laugh out loud.

Then, one by one, Grand Master told us to leave the room. He only held back one of my friends to do a special treatment for him. My friend's family doctor had told him that he had a medical problem. He was afraid that it would turn into an issue, so he asked the Grand Master for help. I told you that I saw one of my friends on the ground sucking that freezing air under the doorway. It was one of the funniest things I had ever seen. Now, I watched my pal hold his butt over the hot, boiling, black cauldron. He was screaming and screaming and praying to GOD to make his firing pain end. I never laughed so hard in all my life. In fact, we all pissed in our pants, for real. Grand Master Mac Dom even laughed and that was rare. Our buddy was our hero that day!

I studied with the Grand Master for a month. He allowed me to photograph his entire collection

I never felt in better health in all my life, than while I was at the Grand Master's house. All we ate was organic and fresh foods. My stress was gone, my cancer was gone, and I learned so much about being one with humanity and nature. When I finally presented "My Ask" to the Grand

Master, he had me drink a horrible tasting herbal tea.

When I returned to New Jersey, Colleen and I spent a few weeks going over what I had learned. We talked about how I was going to apply the lessons and values that I learned into my everyday life. We traveled to Hawaii that year and had the time of our lives. We had incredible quality times during that vacation. When life gets hard, I go back to my happy place and that was in Hawaii, alone with my wife Colleen.

Three months after my experience with Grand Master, I received a phone call from him. A call from the Grand Master was rare. He said, "Tonight, there is a high moon that will pass Venus. I am sure you will have a baby boy. You will have four baby boys in your life."

My father Michael and mother Frances holding their grandson, Michael Jr.

We had our first son Michael -- "Mikey "Attardi Jr. on April 6, 2003. It was one of the greatest days of my life. My mother and father were so proud. It was one of Colleen's and my greatest achievements ever. Our Doctor even allowed me to pull Mikey out. That was an experience that my wife and I will never forget.

Being a father is the greatest accomplishment that any man can achieve in their lifetime. It was once all about me. Then I met my wife and it was all about us. Now it was all about our new child. It's funny how life can take you in a completely different direction and bring you into a new way of thinking. When our first son was born, I worked even harder to leave him a legacy that he would be proud of someday.

ACT III
A Broken Heart that Needs Healing

I was thankful for all my blessings. I was married to Colleen, the girl that I loved. I had a son and was a father. My musical collaboration with Dani was extraordinary. My sports publication was very successful. My family was healthy and I was living the dream.

My Father, Michael and I at my wedding in 1999

Then everything changed in 2004. My father went into the hospital for an elective surgery. We were told it would be a minor surgery to repair his neck. He needed a reconstruction bone fusion. It was from an injury that he had gotten during the time he was in the U.S. Army. He never really complained too much about his pain. That generation never complained too much about anything.

After the surgery, the hospital staff had mixed up my father's strict, liquid dietary orders. The staff fed him solid foods instead of a liquid diet. My father aspirated and the food he ate went into his lungs. He spent several months in rehab. He was also a patient at four different hospitals because we were trying to find a doctor who could help him cure his infections. During this time, my father also made me his power of attorney. I was in charge of making all the medical decisions on his behalf. His health was deteriorating. It was not looking good for him.

I read to my father often while he was at Monmouth Medical Center. One night I was reading to him from the new book that I was writing about being a field goal kicker. My father stopped me in the middle of a sentence and said, "You're not doing what you should be doing. You need to tell your stories. Forget about the paper, tell your original stories." I replied, "Dad, I make a great living. I married the most beautiful girl in the world, who gave me my first son. I made 40% profits on all my stocks. We bought a beautiful home in Middletown on the Jersey Shore. My wife and I both have nice cars and we have money saved in the bank. How can you say that I don't know what I am doing?"

He replied, "Everything you mentioned, except for your wife and son, are THINGS! You are better than selling advertising for a sports publication. Tell your stories!" I thought the pain killers were getting to him. Then later that night I sat up until four o'clock in the morning thinking about what my father had said. I promised myself that day that I would do as he said and start telling my stories. I didn't know how I was going to do it but I just start writing.

A few days later, doctors said that my father had to get his legs amputated because of Gangrene. How did he get gangrene? He became a severe diabetic while he was in the hospital. The trial drugs had spiked his diabetes so high that the infection was not healing and he became septic. I was the one who told him. He listened, and then said in a stern voice. "I was born with two legs and I will leave this earth with two legs!" I knew, he meant it. My father did not have to say something to me twice. I was raised to pay attention and listen.

I begged my father to change his mind about his legs, but he was serious that he did not want to have his legs amputated. He said, "I made you my power of attorney because I know that your mother and sisters will not be able to carry out my wishes. They will let those doctors cut my legs off. I need you to step up like the man I know you to be. A man of your word."

Everyone was begging me to have the doctors amputate his legs. It was the hardest decision I ever had to make in my life. My hero just asked me to let him die. I made him a promise that has haunted me ever since. My father went into a coma that night. I held his hand until his last breath and the last beat of his heart had stopped at 5:10 AM. I never cried so hard in my life. Thank God, my mother was there to help me.

At the young age of 70, my father died on June 19, 2004 at the Hospice Center at Monmouth Medical Center, Long Branch. He was born in Neptune, he resided in Long Branch for 68 years. My father served with the U.S. Army from 1954-1962 as an Army SP4 for the Military Police. He was honored with four military medals.

He attended Valley Forge Military Academy, where he was named to the All-American Football Team in 1954. He was also elected to the Long Branch Athletic Hall of Fame for football in 1984. He received full U.S. Army Military burial honors that took place at Brig. General William C. Doyle Veterans Memorial Cemetery, Arnytown, New Jersey.

My father loved the City of Long Branch. When he made the Long Branch
Hall of Fame for football during my senior year of high school,
I was never so proud of his accomplishment.

At my father's funeral, my family asked me to read the elegy and eulogy. I told the story about the time when my sister Michelle asked me to climb up the attic ladder to get her Barbie dolls. As I was climbing up the old ladder, Michelle turned off the lights, shut the door and began laughing. I couldn't see and I slipped and fell to the bottom.

Michelle had heard the loud crash from me falling. She pushed opened the door and tried to help me up. Then she noticed that I had blood dripping from my fingertips. I was embarrassed that I fell and I pushed her away. She grabbed me and turned me around to see where the blood was coming from. Then she let out a blood curdling scream.

My parents were in the other room with their friends having a fondue party. My father heard her scream and rushed to the attic doorway and grabbed my arm to put pressure on it. I didn't know that I had landed on a razor blade paint scraper. It was hanging next to the ladder I had fallen from. My mother saw all the blood and almost fainted. I still had no idea what had happened because the razor cut was so fine. I was beginning to feel dizzy with the loss of blood.

My father took a towel and wrapped it tightly around my arm and drove

My father was my best friend and we had a lot of fun together

me to the hospital. When the doctor was putting stitches in my arm my father distracted me. He said, "Did you learn anything tonight?" In pain I responded, "Yes, I will never go up to the attic again." My father said, "No, boys should never play with dolls! That's the lesson." The nurse and even the doctor started to laugh as he was sewing two rows of stitches in my arm. The experience was painful. My father's quick humor: priceless!

30 things my father, Michael J. Attardi, used to say to me:

1) A successful man is one who is loved and respected by his family and friends.

2) An education is something no one can ever take away from you; then again, a Super Bowl ring would be pretty hard to pry off my fingers.

3) A foolish man speaks as a wise man will listen. You will never learn anything from hearing yourself talk. Do you hear what I'm saying?

4) The truth always comes out, so always tell the truth.

5) Never underestimate your dreams. They'll come true if you work at them.

6) Always look people in the eyes when you're talking to them.

7) If you work hard, don't forget to play hard. You must have a balance.

8) Never bite the hand that feeds you, especially if their serving you lobsters.

9) It's alright to dream just don't find yourself caught in a nightmare.

10) When you read a book, try to understand the real message, not just the words.

11) I love you for loving me.

12) The water is never too calm; tell that to the man who got eaten by the shark.

13) Treat your girlfriends like you would want a boy to treat your sisters. With respect!

14) When you talk about yourself, no one really wants to listen. People listen when it comes from someone else, so stop talking about you and listen to me. Be humble!

15) I never lived a day I didn't like.

16) Live each day as if it were your last, maybe then you could finally hit a curve ball.

17) If you give up your dream, you die, not of the flesh, but of the mind.

18) I would never push you to do anything you didn't want to do; now go and take the garbage out.

19) You were great in that show, I didn't understand it, but you were great.

20) If you're going to do something, then give it all you've got. Don't half ass it.

21) Do you know why you're going to make it? Cause you don't care what others think.

22) Don't let your heart control your future. Listen to it, react to it, and then move onto common sense.

23) Always, always have a nice pair of shoes. People judge you by your shoes.

24) Do you know that saying; never look a gift horse in the mouth?

Dad with a family friend Dominick Nittolo acting like "The Fonz".

Good news, you'll never have to worry about it because we don't own horses.

25) If life gives you lemons, sell them. Buy apples and make an apple pie. Apple pies taste much better then lemonade trust me.

26) Humility is the essence of life.

27) I have never been so proud of you in my whole life. I'm honored to call you my son.

28) You will never get rid of me because I live inside of you and your kids will know who I was. I just know that about you, you're a special one. You're like a super hero.

29) Treat everyone with respect, love and kindness, then someday it will return back to you and the cycle goes on and on.

30) Always cherish your mother; she made me do it for 35 years, so now it's your turn.

There is not a day that goes by that I don't think about my father. I bought a grandfather clock and placed a brass nameplate with this name, Mike - "Iron Mike"- Attardi 3/6/1934. My sons and I wind up that clock every week. It chimes every 15 minutes and it plays the most beautiful songs on the hour. It is our reminder that he still lives inside of me and my three sons. It is one of my most cherished material things in my life. I was not around for my father's birth, but I held him during his death. We all miss you Dad.

Divine Intervention

The death of my father took a heavy toll on my health. All that I had learned from the Grand Master was put aside as if it never happened. The only thing I continued to do was to drink that horrible herbal tea. I woke up in a cold sweat the night we buried my father. It was almost like he was speaking to me from his grave. I began to have dreams about musical melodies. I would wake up in the middle of the night writing songs and musical scores. I have always said that my song writing was divine intervention.

It became my nightly ritual to get out of bed and sing new songs into a portable mini-tape recorder. These recorders were the same ones that doctors or lawyers would use to dictate letters. I would write two or three songs a night. Colleen would hear me and wake up. After a while, she got used to waking up and finding me working until morning. Colleen said, "Are you working on another song?"

Twin Treasures was my first Off-Broadway Show

My wife thought I was going crazy, but every morning I would share my new music with her. She was always surprised at what I had done.

Once again, we called it divine intervention. I still can't explain how over 100 songs came to me during my sleep.

Dani and I were still collaborating on original musical compositions for "Twin Treasures." Kit Stolen was one of my movie making partners, too. We wrote and created the off-Broadway Musical of "Twin Treasures." It was an off-Broadway hit! We received rave reviews from several musical theater critics. We were very pleased.

I had the most fascinating, hardworking cast and crew

The show was first performed at the Strand Theater in Lakewood, New Jersey, on April 2, 2005. It was the same day Pope John Paul passed away. The show went on for three weekends with rave reviews. We went on to win the Perry Awards for Best New Song and Best New Musical. Dani and I also won an award for the Best New Song, "Wish upon a Star Tonight."

We were elated and humbled by the success of "Twin Treasures." We were so inspired that we knew we had to keep writing and turn the musical into an animation short movie. That show kicked off the start of my animation company. We thought that we had found gold with this project!

I was asked by an interviewer from Variety Magazine, "How could I create the music I did, if I wasn't formally trained?" My honest response,

This show was my way to help heal the loss of my father

"Divine Intervention." I did have a little bit of training. I took one semester studying music composition at Westminster Chorus College in Princeton, New Jersey. I had a love for melodies and music structure. I learned a lot being around Dani and musicians all my life. My father always said, "Surround yourself with smarter people than yourself." If Walt Disney can do it, I could do it I thought.

In a matter of a month, I had composed over 125 original songs. I also began working on them in Orlando, Florida with Dani. This was an exciting time for me. I felt that I had a higher calling to share my work with the world. I could fund our new musical venture with the money I made from the sports publication.

Dani and I had something magical happening and we never wanted to question it. We would work on our music for several days in a row, not even stopping for something to eat. That is how motivated and serious we were about creating our new soundtracks. I remember Dani and me working through four major hurricanes in 2004. Hurricane's Charley, Frances, Ivan and Jeanne. Every time the power would go out, we would run outside and turn on the gas generator. Power would come back up and we would be working again. Nothing was going to stop us at that point.

Not even category 4 hurricanes!

Dani and I completed four soundtracks for my animated films. Each soundtrack had at least twenty-two song tracks. In three months, we created eighty-eight demo songs. These songs would become the blueprints for my animated screenplays. The music had inspired me to write a story around the music that we had created. I had no idea if this was the proper way to create a musical until I read an article about Alan Menken and Howard Ashman.

Menken and Ashman were contacted by Jeffery Katzenberg to work with Disney on The Little Mermaid, yet there was no completed script. Menken and Ashman sent several songs to Katzenberg. Katzenberg stopped the writers until they heard all the songs. Their songs were instrumental to the Disney writers. Later, John Muster and Ron Clements created the masterpiece that we know today.

The poster for the musical Twin Treasures.

Hurricane Wilma in Cozumel

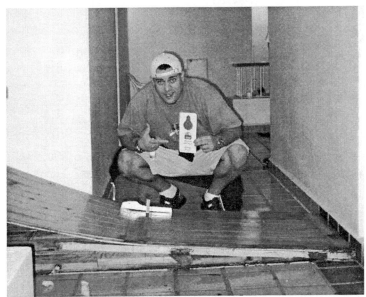

This was our hotel room door that was blown off its hinges.
Not even my do not disturb sign could help.

My father-in-law Richard and I became certified SCUBA divers in November 2004 after my father's death. It was something I always wanted to do and it seemed like a great escape. The ocean was my love and the thought of being able to be one with nature excited me. It was almost like going back home.

We went to this big SCUBA diving show in North Jersey called Beneath the Sea. During that show, we both took a chance on a raffle ticket for a free trip to Cozumel. The trip included airfare, hotel and SCUBA diving adventures. I wanted to win the trip! I knew if we did, we would have the time of our lives. They drew the ticket and called our number. We had the winning number! We were never so happy knowing that we were going to have a whole week in Cozumel, SCUBA diving in paradise.

We decided to take our trip in October 2005. When we arrived, we found ourselves at the Hotel Cozumel that was located on the shoreline. We went to our hotel and decided to wait a few hours before we got into the water for our first shoreline dive. The next day, we completed a drift dive class and dove the Santa Rosa Wall. The famous oceanographer Jacques Yves Cousteau came to Cozumel in 1961. He brought his crew on the Calypso to film a documentary. When the film aired, Cozumel went to the top of diving lists for the best diver's destinations in the world.

There are vast coral heads, brilliant sponges, hundreds of tropical fish, rich ecosystems and steep walls that sink into the abyss. There are also tunnels and caves that twist through the reef. They provide a rich environment for many species, including some not found anywhere else on earth. We were excited when we found an underwater grotto. It was the same grotto that had inspired the animators for the animated feature, The Little Mermaid. How serendipity is that?

When we got back to shore, a few of the locals told us that a hurricane was heading our way. Immediately, we went back to the hotel to find out what some of our options were. I called Continental Airlines and they told us that we were not able to fly out that night. I even called Congressman Frank Pallone's office to see if there would be any way he could help get us out that night. With no way out, we decided to stay and weather the storm. How bad can a hurricane be? I went through four hurricanes with Dani only a year ago.

The very next day, was the most incredible day ever. There wasn't a cloud in the sky and the water was crystal blue and green. There was a local attraction called the Dolphin Experience. It was located right on the ocean. The dolphin trainers asked if we could help move their dolphins into our large hotel swimming pool. It was necessary for their safety. There I was with others, placing eight dolphins in gurneys. Then we transferred them from their pool into our hotel's pool.

Everything in Cozumel looked peaceful for the moment. I guess the dolphins made us happy and eased our concerns about a hurricane that was not yet in sight. But, three hours later, the sky appeared dark and menacing. It looked like a scene from the movie Harry Potter, when Lord Voldemort showed up with the dark sky. The sky I was looking at was the darkest that I had ever seen in my life. This was the start of Hurricane Wilma. And it was heading straight for us.

Before the storm hit us, I had called my friend Dominic Ambrosia from HBO, who gave me the phone number for CNN. Then I called and spoke to a news producer who hired me on the spot. Then she connected me with a live CNN reporter who would be my contact. I was CNN's on location reporter in Cozumel. My job was to keep in contact with them and to give them the information needed for them to cover the story. Two "old school" wall pay phones were the only phones working at that time. All the cellular phone service was down. So, I purchased over $500 worth of calling cards from the gift shop.

My Father-in-law Richard "Dick" Cole-Hatchard after Wilma hit

The raging storm hit us hard that afternoon. There was destruction everywhere. The hurricane tore down several hotels on the shoreline. It demolished the beautiful seashore city to rubble.

We took shelter in the basement of our hotel. We had several lines of people with buckets, scooping out water so that we would have a place to sleep that night. The wind was howling. It sounded like 10,000 cats whining at the same time. It was one of the scariest sounds I've ever heard up till this day.

I didn't know if our hotel was going to be the next one to be hit. If we did get hit, we'd be under a pile of concrete, so I moved our group of people into an area that was much safer. The storm hovered over us for 24 hours. By the middle of the following afternoon, it looked like a bomb had hit our hotel. Large sections of concrete were tossed all over our front lobby. Hurricane Wilma destroyed everything in its path.

I found a public telephone in the hotel hallway that had been ripped off the wall and was lying on the floor. I remembered my grandfather at that moment. He was an incredible carpenter and he had taught me a lot about electrical wiring. I saw a faintly, lit light flickering on the phone. I knew, I had an opportunity to use the phone to communicate with CNN. I worked on that phone for over an hour, splicing wires together and making sure that I could get a signal. It was one of the most tedious jobs I'd ever attempted, but I knew I had to do something if we're going to get any help.

Cozumel was turned into rubble after Hurricane Wilma hit us.

I got a dial tone and used my calling card to dial CNN. This time I was talking with Anderson Cooper, live on CNN News. The transcripts still can be seen online. I spoke to Anderson Cooper four different times during CNN news segments. I reported the troubles and tribulations we were experiencing and how we needed to get out of Mexico. I had to disconnect the wires every time we talked. I didn't want anyone to figure out how I was calling out. I felt like MacGyver. Only he would have built a plane and got out of there a day ago. It was a serious situation and people were scared. We did not have water, food or medicine. We had no security to back up the 125 American citizens that had migrated to the Hotel Cozumel for safety.

I was talking to Anderson Cooper without the Mexican Government's consent. They were not happy when they found out. They sent over sensors to find out who Michael Attardi was and how he was communicating with CNN news. The Mexican Official Sensor arrived. He asked us only one question, "Who is Michael Attardi?" All the men that were in that large room, raised their hand. One by one, they were saying that they were Mike Attardi. It was like a scene out of a Hollywood movie. I was grateful to them. But, I never was so scared. I was holding my breath as I held up my hand as well.

The sensor finally left the room. Later that night, I found my torn up public telephone and spliced the wires. I got a dial tone and called CNN. I told Anderson Cooper the entire story on national TV. The next morning, large white vans picked all the 125 American citizens up at the Hotel Cozumel. They drove us to the Cozumel airport. When we arrived at the airport, it was like a mob scene. Every American that was trying to leave that island was waiting at the gates. There were hundreds of armed national guardsmen from Mexico there too. They stood with their machine guns guarding the airport.

I had a brilliant idea but I needed to get to the person in charge of opening that airport gate. There were two linebacker-type guys in my group that directed me all the way to the front of the line. When I got there, I pulled out my passport. I had placed my old U.S. Congressional sticker seal to my passport holder many years ago. I showed it to the head guardsmen. I told him that I needed to get all my people on the next plane or we will have an international incident. I kept flashing my congressional sticker at him like it was an important badge.

He went over to talk with his superiors. We waited. Then the heavily armed soldiers came back. One of them handed me back my ID while another one opened the gate. I got all the 125 American citizens onto the next Continental Airlines flight. When we were on the airplane taking off, a roar of cheers, cries and laugher filled the cabin of our airplane. Several hands were patting my shoulders and thanking me. I wanted to get out of there as badly as they did. I stayed focused and always knew that I was going to get us all out safely.

I could not believe that a simple sticker had worked or they just wanted Mike Attardi out of their country. I was just happy to get everyone onto that plane. We had children, we had seniors and all different types of people on the airplane. We had United States citizens wanting to go back home to their loved ones. That was the most important thing to me. Not to forget to mention that my wife, mother-in -law Sandy and my son were all waiting for us in Florida.

When I met up with my family in Orlando, Florida they were ecstatic to see us as much as we were to see them. That very trip, I would learn that God had blessed Colleen and me once again. I was very excited to learn that we were having our second son. We welcomed Nathaniel on July 8, 2006. Talk about your game changers.

Tom Hanks and Winning 96 Awards

The Cover of Shore Living Magazine

In 2006, I met David Ciambrone who owned a local Italian restaurant. David and I decided to set up investor meetings for us to start a local production company. David is a great guy. He would give you the shirt off his back. David and I met Joe Anselmo, a real-estate broker who had a true love and passion for film. Joe and David believed that I had the talent to be a successful writer/director. They both believed in me.

They raised over 100 thousand dollars in less than four months. My friends and family and an investor named Matt Phillips also helped. We were now able to make a short-animated film. If it wasn't for Matt, David and Joe, this film would have never been made. Matt is a kind and gentle man who also believed in my talents as a filmmaker. My only regret was not being able to get our feature film completed. I found myself not wanting to make the film for me, but for Matt, Joe and David. That is how much I love and respect these men.

Joe, David, Matt and I continued to work together. We also worked with an animation school located in the back of Universal Studios. We produced an animated short film called, "Once Upon a Christmas Village." The film was unique. It was one of the first times that 3D CGI animation was used with live action backgrounds using a Boris scope lens and Red Camera.

Directing our short animation film at Universal Studios

The process took extra time because we had to make sure that the shadowing and lighting were perfect. You must be conscious about continuity to achieve a marriage with the two worlds of animation and live action. That is why Walt Disney films are so special. It was all about their attention on detail, which we all believed in.

It was the little details that took a film from just being an animation film into a great animated movie. There are three key ingredients of all storytelling: story, story and story. If your story is weak, no matter what the animation looks like, people will not gravitate towards it.

I had this crazy idea of wanting to use the actors Tim Curry and Jim Belushi. I sent the script and music to Tim's agent in Hollywood. Marcia

Hurwitz was Curry's voice agent and she kept returning my script back as unsolicited.

I turned to Joe and told him that I had an idea about how we could get the script to Marcia Hurwitz. When I was recovering from cancer, I worked for Federal Express as a driver. After my employment with FedEx ended, I kept the uniform to use as a possible Halloween costume. Joe and I got on a plane and went out to Los Angeles.

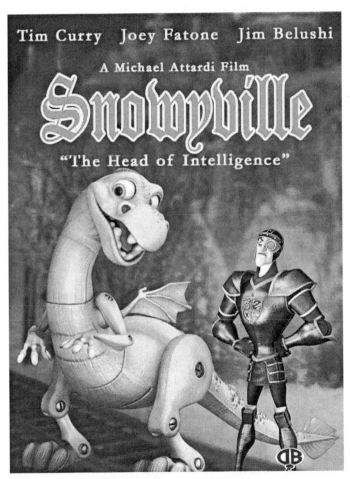

Tim Curry   Joey Fatone   Jim Belushi

A Michael Attardi Film

Snowyville

"The Head of Intelligence"

Once Upon a Christmas Village turns into Snowyville

I put on my FedEx uniform and showed up at Innovative Artist Company and asked for Mrs. Hurwitz. At first, the staff didn't understand why they couldn't just sign for it. When I walked in her office, I handed her the FedEx package. She opened it and saw that it was the same script that she kept sending back. Marcia looked at me and said, "You're not the FedEx guy are you"? I replied, "No, I'm the writer/director who wants Tim Curry to be the voice of Sir Evil."

She looked at me and smiled. "You wait here." At that time, I was looking for an exit in case she was calling the police. Instead, Marcia called in some of the other agents and asked them, "Who is this?" as she was pointing at me. Most of them answered the obvious, "The FedEx guy". "No, this is Michael Attardi, a writer/director who has been sending me his script for two months."

Dani Donadi and Tim Curry in London, England at Recording Studio

They all looked at me in disbelief. Then she said to her staff: "If you had courage like he does, we would be a lot more successful here. Now get back to work!" Marcia turned to me and said, "Who do you want for your film?" I was a little bashful when I said, "Tim Curry. "You got him! Who else?" "Jim Belushi" I replied. Marcia picked up the phone and called Jim Belushi's people and the deal was done in minutes. She then asked me, "Can you be in London tomorrow? Tim is working on Spamalot and the show opens in two weeks. He's in rehearsals. Tim has only tomorrow open in his schedule."

I took a flight to Orlando, picked up Dani and we flew on a Virgin Atlantic flight that same night. We arrived early the next morning and went to Jungle Recording Studio in London. Dani and I were still dragging our luggage behind us. Each one of us only had one of our eyes open. We were both exhausted and wanted to sleep.

We turned down a long alley leading to the music studio. Outside the studio, Tim Curry was smoking a cigarette. I stopped in front of Tim and said, "Mr. Curry, you're my hero." Curry laughed as he said, "Anyone who makes a deal in Hollywood, gets on an airplane and drags their carcass over here on one days' notice is my hero.

Working with our crew on our short film.

Come on boys, let's go have some fun." Dani and I followed him into the studio like two happy kids. We felt like we met Willy Wonka and he was taking us into his chocolate factory. We had so much fun recording, that he invited us to Oktoberfest in Germany.

Dani and I came home from that unbelievable experience with great memories. In fact, there is not a time that we don't remind each other of the events that transpired from that trip. Let's just say, there was a lot of beer drinking going on in Germany. We needed that after the travels we endured that week.

Dani and I returned home for only a few days. Then we were on the move again. We flew out to Los Angeles to record Jim Belushi at a recording studio in Santa Monica. Joe came out with me and Dani. We visited Marcia and had dinner at Lobsters on Santa Monica Pier. That is where we met our waiter, Mickey.

Mickey had a deep strong voice. When he first talked to us, I looked at Joe and said "He's our Dragasauras. We signed Mikey that night and he did his voice-over work with Jim Belushi the next day. Belushi was so impressed with Mickey that he thought he was a voice-over actor for years. Never would we have told Jim that we met him last night in a restaurant and he was our waiter. How cliché even for Hollywood standards.

Jim Belushi, Joe Anselmo, Dani Donadi and I
at the recording studio in Santa Monica, CA

Belushi spent a lot of time with us making sure that his voice-over takes were perfect. Jim even shared a few stories about how he got started in the business. His uncle owned a hamburger place in Chicago. It was the same hamburger place that his brother, John, created a skit about with Dan Aykroyd on Saturday Night Live.

His uncle that owned that burger place told Jim that he should be doing what his brother John is doing, acting. His uncle handed him a Santa Claus outfit and hired him to play Santa for the customers. That was his very first acting job. When he read my script, he fell in love with the harshness and truthfulness that my Santa Claus had. He told us that was the only reason why he agreed to accept the job. That and he also heard about the FedEx outfit.

He later asked, "Why does Tim Curry get to sing a song and my character doesn't?" I looked at Dani and turned back to Belushi and said "We will have a song for you. Can we lay it down after lunch?" He agreed and we all took a half an hour break.

With Tim Curry at a film festival in Florida

Dani and I franticly started to write in the studio. We borrowed a keyboard and hooked it into the midi and started to compose a melody. I wrote the melody and lyrics in less than 10 minutes and we had a song. Belushi returned from lunch and we taught him the song. He loved the song and he only needed one take. That's all we did was one take.

It was like the music gods rained down their magic onto us once again. Dani and I wrote a song for Jim Belushi in less than 10 minutes and recorded it in one take. It was insane! When it was time to leave Los Angeles, we knew that we had something special.

We finished the 15-minute short animated film on December 10, 2006. We submitted the film to the Festival De Cannes. Our film was denied. That same week we received an invitation to show our film at the

Washington, DC Film Festival.

The film was being shown at the University of the District of Columbia. The same University I studied at when I was working on Capitol Hill in 1990. The film festival director knew who I was. He loved the film so much that he highlighted it during the short-animated film competition. Our unknown film beat out two Academy Award Nominated Short Animated films. We won Best Short Film Animation. The news of our win in Washington, DC sent out shockwaves in the film festival circuit.

Joe and I began receiving invitations from some of the major film festivals in the country. Then out of nowhere, the Festival De Cannes offered us a spot. We would be competing in the Short Animation Moving Pictures competition. I walked the Red Carpet at the Festival De Cannes on May 21, 2007. I remember thinking to myself as the camera lights were flashing, "How the hell did I get here?" I have always wanted to walk the Red Carpet at the Festival De Cannes.

Walking the Red Carpet at the Festival De Cannes

The only one who was missing was Joe Anselmo. They only allowed me to have one Red Carpet ticket. As much as I wanted Joe to share the glory, they would not allow him a ticket. Our relationship after that festival was never the same.

That was one of my biggest regrets in business. I was not able to keep the magic that Joe, David, Matt and I created with that one animated short film. They will always have a special place in my heart. They all believed in me when others said no. I have so much respect for them.

Once Upon a Christmas won 96 Awards from 2007-08. Making it the most awarded independent short film of all-time.
Hard work and asking for things made that film a success.

When I got back from France, I went to Los Angeles to meet a few producers. One of my friends insisted that I join him for dinner that night. We met at this old-time restaurant where Frank Sinatra, Dean Martin and Sammy Davis, Jr. used to eat. To my surprise and shock, we sat down to have dinner with Tom Hanks and several others. I shook Tom's hand and sat back to listen to the conversation.

I could not believe I was with Tom Hanks having dinner. I said only a few words and listened like I was a fly on the wall. That was one of the most magical nights in my life. Tom Hanks would never know who I was, even if he saw me later that night in a police line-up. That's how quiet I was. I remember my father saying, "A wise man listens and the idiot likes to talk." I saw Tom once again a few years later at the screening for Saving Mr. Banks. As I suspected, he didn't know who the hell I was even when I explained that we met before. That's ok, I still managed to get my wife his autograph. He'll always be one of my favorite actors of all-time!

Meeting the Sopranos

Colleen and I used to watch the hit show *The Sopranos* on HBO. We loved that show. We loved that everyone watching was cheering for the villain. Tony Soprano was an American hero and you wanted to see him succeed. Some of the Soprano characters were so legendary because lesser-known actors were made into huge stars in everyday conversations.

With Actor James Gandolfini and Diane Raver at the Garden State Film Festival

We took our film to the Garden State Film festival. Director Diane Raver called me and said that I needed to meet her at the Asbury Park Convention Hall at 2 p.m. I agreed and met Diane. To my surprise, Diane introduced me to actor James Gandolfini, who played Tony Soprano in the hit show The Sopranos. James took the time to talk to me and he had some great advice. James said," You should write a book about your life and make a movie out of it." Thank you, James. I think I will.

When we were taking my short film out to the festival circuit, I was invited to attend the Italian-American film festival in New York City. This festival meant so much to me since I was an American-Italian who had just made an animation film. It was also incredible because the directors of the festival made me feel like I was part of the family because they were all Italian.

With Actor/Artist Federico Castelluccio in Los Angeles at the International film market shopping our film Numba One.

I took my mother and sister to the event and we went to a little Italian restaurant near the venue. We had finished our coffee and walked outside of the restaurant. I turned around to see what direction we needed to go and Federico Castelluccio who played the role of Furio Giunta, was walking towards us. My mother and sister both were in shock. In unison, they both said: "Holy crap! That is Fuiro from The Sopranos!" I moved towards Federico and put out my hand to introduce myself. Federico was very gracious and was used to people coming up to him in New York City. I told him that I was a fan of The Sopranos and we exchanged a handshake.

Then I introduced my mother and sister who were getting a bit excited to meet him. I said, "These two crazy ladies want to meet you." Federico replied, "I like crazy ladies." We laughed. I told him that I was in New York because my animated film was being shown at the Italian Film Festival. Coincidently, he told us that his film was in the same festival and that is where he was headed. We all started to walk down the street together towards the venue. I've been around rockstars in my day, but when we were walking with Federico in New York City for those several blocks, everyone on that street knew who he was. Shouts from fans, "We love you Furio!"

We all showed up at the festival and watched all the winning films from the festival. Both of our films were featured as best in show. Federico came up to me after he saw my film, Once Upon a Christmas Village. He was impressed and intrigued by my style of animation because it was so different. He noticed that I used live action backgrounds with animation. Not too many filmmakers were doing that kind of animation back then. After the festival, we all went out to dinner and talked about possible projects that we could work on together. Federico treated me like I had been one of his best friends for years, that's the kind a guy he is. I was excited because I finally found another artist who understood what I was trying to do with my animation. Everyone back then was trying to make realistic animation, while I was trying to make it raw and organic. I learned that from Walt Disney, Jim Henson and Chuck Jones. If your story is strong, the medium you use to make it does not have to be overshadowing. Federico got it.

I know, people who watched The Sopranos would think differently about Federico, but I got to know the person that he really is and not the character he portrayed. We continued to talk about art, music and animation. We kept in touch and found out that we had a lot more in common than we thought. A few weeks later, we hung out a couple of times in New York City. One night we were invited to the one-man show of The Bronx Tale with Chazz Palminteri. Federico and Chazz were close friends. It was a real honor to be Federico's guest. That night we had dinner and a lot of laughs with Chazz. Both of them are great story tellers.

A month later there was a film festival in Bucks County, Pennsylvania. Federico and I were invited by my friend, Hayden Craddolph, to show our films and to speak on a panel. During the drive there, I shared with him an idea about a new film called Numba One. Federico loved the concept behind the story of this mafia romantic comedy. He encouraged me to start writing the script and a month later, I sent him the first draft. Federico thought it was one of the funniest scripts that he had read in a long time and really wanted to help me make it into a movie.

When Colleen and I had our third son, Matthew, we asked Federico and my sister Francine to be his godparents. We had a beautiful celebration at St. Michael's Church in Long Branch, New Jersey. We decided to bring the whole family up from Florida so we could spend it with our family in New Jersey for Matthew's Christening.

My wife Colleen, our son Matthew, Federico and my sister Francine

Federico is one of the most talented fine artists that I know and is a real stand-up guy. Not only is he a true friend and someone I care about very deeply, but he's also like the brother that I never had. I could write a book about all the fun we have shared together. To this day, Federico and his fiancé Yvonne Schaefer and I are still trying to make the movie Numba One.

The Last of Walt Disney's Nine Old Men

On August 19, 2008, I traveled to Southern California: I went to Hollywood....

The official invitation I had received for Ollie Johnston's Life Celebration.

I had the privilege to be invited to one of the most important events in my animation career. It was the Ollie Johnston Life Celebration-Good Ol' Tinsel Town. The Sunset Avenue sidewalks were filled with advertising peddlers wearing eBay costumes of Bugs Bunny and SpongeBob. There was also endless food courts and faux-trendy boutiques. Hollywood is a theme park of broken dreams, where actors from all over the world come to be waiters and waitresses.

There are very few events that could draw me away from Orlando, Florida. A tribute to Ollie Johnston, the last of "Walt Disney's Nine Old

Men," was one such an event. I would have traveled to the ends of the world to be part of this special life celebration. That is how much the "Nine Old Men" meant to me and my career. Up to this point, I had only met four of "Walt Disney's Nine Old Men," a name invented by Walt Disney himself. These nine men were his most talented and trusted animators at Disney.

The invitation-only affair was held at Disney's El Capitan Theatre. It's a beautifully remodeled venue that gestures back to the 1930's golden age of animation. Hollywood was a cultural center for a new form of entertainment, rather than just another must to do stop for busloads of curious world tourists.

The event's host, Leonard Maltin, took the stage. From the start, it was clear that this evening would be different than virtually every other presentation on Disney animation that I've ever attended. The event entailed animators talking to animators. It was assumed that everyone in the audience knew the difference between a rough and clean-up drawing. It was also assumed that the audience knew the difference between the era of ink-and-paint and the era of Xerox. Some presenters even assumed that the audience could tell the difference between a series of drawings chiseled out by Disney animator Milt Kahl and a similar series of drawings that Ollie Johnston whispered onto the page. No computer talks here.

The four-hour presentation was thematically divided into the three areas of Ollie's life: his home life, his life as an artist and animator, and his lifelong interest in steam trains. Ollie's two sons, Rick and Ken, told stories about their father at home and at the studio. Rick recalled that a childhood photograph of himself, in which he was holding his ear and sucking his thumb, became the inspiration for a sequence in "Robin Hood" in which Prince John adopts a similar pose.

Ken also told the story of accompanying Ollie to the White House in 2005, where he was the first animator to receive the National Medal of Arts. The most touching aspect of the experience, according to Ken, was

Ollie Johnston, Frank Thomas, Ward Kimble, Milt Kahl and Marc Davis

not the medal, rather the moment in which his father told President Bush that he loved him.

Disney Historian, Leonard Maltin was also a speaker. He introduced a few men who shared Ollie's lifelong enthusiasm for steam trains. Then Michael Broggie, son of Roger Broggie Sr., took the stage. He worked for Walt Disney, and grew up at the studio. Michael told the story of Ollie's backyard locomotive. Ollie had inspired Walt to build a similar scale railroad in his own backyard. He called it the Carolwood Pacific Railroad. Michael went on to say that without that railroad, there might not have been a Disneyland. There may not have been any Disney theme park as we know them today. His backyard train was the catalyst of his theme park empire.

The discussion of Ollie as master animator was overseen by those artists who came to the studio in the 1970s, such as Glen Keane, John Musker, Ron Clements, John Lasseter and Brad Bird. Together these men not only defined Ollie's philosophical understanding of craft, but also the real-life attention to detail and grace.

The world of animation has changed since Ollie retired from the studio. However, his work and teachings will continue to inspire young animators well into the future. Ollie's brand of character-based animation was a personal type of art. Casual animation observers can recognize the

John Lasseter shares a story about Pixar and the new direction for Disney Animation

Disney Legendary Musical Composer, Richard Sherman- Mary Poppins

Disney Legendary Director, John Musker – The Little Mermaid and Aladdin

Glen Keane recalls what it was like to work under Ollie, the great animation master

difference of Ollie Johnston scenes and others. They can see the difference in a scene drawn by another animator, such as Marc Davis or Ken Anderson.

In Ollie's day, a single animator would oversee an entire scene and sequences of scenes. The artist's idiosyncratic drawing style graced each pose, each movement. Animated sequences in "Pinocchio" and "Fantasia" are a series of unified sequential drawings. They are a synthesis of character and animator, art and artist. The lead animators at Disney and Warner Brothers became celebrities. They weren't just artists contributing to a unified project. They were artists whose individual drawing styles created visual tension on the screen.

In the past 10 or 12 years, I've noticed that the nature of American animation has changed. Computer animation offers stunning detail and camera movement. It limits the ways an individual animator can influence an image on the screen. Computer-based character animation is unified 3D character models, virtual skeletons, and computer-assisted motion. The new animation celebrities are animators. They are also the directors and producers like Brad Bird, Andrew Stanton, and John Lasseter.

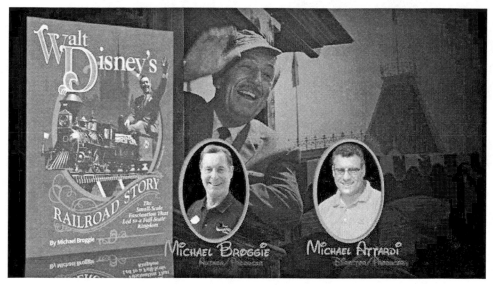

Michael Broggie and I will make this movie someday

The Ollie Johnston Tribute held a double sadness for me. Ollie Johnston was the last of the Walt's Nine Old Men, those animators he most trusted at the studio. The other eight have already passed on. In fact, most all the Disney animators from the 1930s have left us. But the loss of Ollie was greater than that of a single man. It was the loss of a wonderful craft. Only John Lasseter would understand. I have so much respect for John Lasseter. John is our modern-day Walt Disney.

One of the most amazing experiences that night was meeting all the Disney royalty. I say that out of true admiration and respect for their legacy and dedication to Walt and the Disney family. One speaker that night was so inspirational that I had to meet him. His name was Michael Broggie. Michael wrote an extraordinary book titled "Walt Disney's Railroad Story."

Michael Broggie is the son of the first Walt Disney Imagineer, Roger

Broggie. Roger Broggie was the creator of the multi-plane camera. It changed the face of animation film forever. Roger was instrumental in creating animatronics. We have all grown to love this wonderful world of animatronics throughout the Disney Parks.

Roger also helped build the Lilly Belle, which was named after Walt's wife, Lillian Disney. The Lilly Belle was Walt Disney's 1/8 scale train engine. He ran it in his back yard and called it the Carolwood Pacific Railroad.

The stories Michael shared with me that night truly inspired me. I had to speak more with this amazing person. We exchanged information and agreed to keep in touch. We have been working on a film idea for the past several years and we are ready to make it.

Michael and I have spent a lot of time together. He's a true gentleman and showman. He could captivate any crowd with his amazing stories about Walt Disney and the Nine Old Men. His wife Sharon is the salt of the earth. Sharon is an incredible woman who has been by Michael's side for over 40 years. I have learned a great deal from Michael and Sharon. I only wish that Colleen and I have the longevity of love and harmony that they have. Not only are they true friends but also mentors of mine. I respect and love them.

A Dream Balloon Flies Higher

Later that year, I met John Hadity. John was a movie producer with the Weinstein Company and we met at the Nashville Film Festival. We went out in the world to raise the money we needed to make a full-length feature animated film. John knows how to raise money. He's amazing!

The Animated character of Santa played by Jim Belushi helped us win 96 awards that year

I contacted a dear friend of mine, All-Pro football player Phil Villapiano. I asked if he would throw me a meet and greet party at his house with some of his friends who may be interested in investing in the project. Although we had two parties, no one wrote a check except for my cousins Anthony and Linda for 100 thousand dollars.

Phil also contacted a friend of his who lived on the Navesink River. His name was Pat Scire. He made all his money in the financial district before that tragic day of 9-11. Pat agreed to meet with me. After our meeting, he was convinced that I was Walt Disney reincarnated. I only wish! Pat understood what I was trying to do and he knew that I had the passion and love for my trade. He had never invested in a project like this before but he was winning to take the chance because he liked who I was and what I represented. Pat never met too many "Boy Scouts" in his day and I was his new project. Pat was a great supporter and he went out of his way to help.

With the help of Pat and his team of investors, we created Dream Balloon Enterprises. We raised only 1.5 million dollars. However, the company's business plan called for 5 million dollars. To have a successful project you need to raise the full budget. I've learned to never start a business or venture unless you have the full amount of funding and then some. Pat warned me but we kept moving forward anyway.

Artist, Nicolosi, Me, Colleen and Tim Curry at Hayden Film Festival.
Tim made our film an International success.

Then my family and I moved to Windermere, FL in March of 2008. We took a leap of faith with no promises or guarantees. We still had not sold our house in Middletown, New Jersey. During this time, I was talking to new investors. I wanted to make our short film into a full length animated feature film. My wife and I put our money on the line as well.

We created several animated short films to shop to Hollywood. Unfortunately, Hollywood was not buying anything at that time. Everyone was feeling the pinch. Even a few of my investors that were worth millions, were feeling a little cautious about spending money at this time.

I kept the studio up and running for three years on a shoe string budget. We made a few animated commercials and piece work for other projects. We hired an incredible crew of artists. Most of them were trained by Disney and Universal. We had magic going on and everyone believed in us and what we were doing. We worked every day from 9:00 o'clock in the morning to midnight, trying to create the magic and to make that studio work.

The Brian Henson Experiment

With Brian Henson at the Jim Henson Company in Hollywood, CA

I asked Pat Garrett, a very dear friend of mine, to make a call to Brian Henson. Brian is the son of Jim Henson and was running the Jim Henson Company. Pat was the chorographer for the Henson's Muppets Christmas Carol. As fate plays out, a few weeks later, I received a call from actor, Tim Curry. He explained that he just saw Once Upon a Christmas Village for the first time. He thought it was a genius piece of work. Tim sent the film to Brian Henson, and I met Brian in March of 2008.

I received a letter from Brian Henson a week after we met. His letter was very touching. In his letter, he compared me with his father and my heart stopped for a moment. Jim Henson was a hero and inspiration to me. I grew up on Kermit and Miss Piggy. Jim Henson was the real reason that I married animation with live action backgrounds. Jim did that with puppets, using live action backgrounds and a cast of puppets.

As soon as I arrived in Hollywood I walked through the gates of the old A&M recording studio. This studio is where the Jim Henson Company is located. When I walked into Brian Henson's office I got a little nervous. Brian looked at me and asked, if I was okay.

I looked around at all the Emmy Awards, Academy Awards and Telly

Awards. There was also an abundant of Muppet collectibles that any true Henson fan would faint over. Once again, I hear that little voice in my head saying, "Michael, how the hell did you get here?"

Brian said, "I saw your Christmas film and it has a lot of potential. I would like to read the script and get a better grasp on the characters and the full-length story." I did not respond at first. I was still in awe of where I was.

His office was truly magical. I said, "I feel like I have been in his office before. I can't get this feeling out of my head." Brian laughed and said, "This was Charlie Chaplin's old office." I sat down on Brian's leather couch and looked at him with complete disbelief. "Did you say Charlie Chaplin?" If this was not fate or destiny or the universe giving me what I asked for, then I am not able to explain how I was there.

I said, "My grandfather was a stunt double for Charlie Chaplin." I used to carry a photocopy of a photo of him dressed like Chaplin in my daily planner. I pulled out the photo and handed it to Brian. He was also fascinated to hear my story. I was in the same office that my grandfather was in during the 1920's. I am a true believer in fate. I was meant to be here and Brian agreed. We then had a wonderful conversation about his father and how he started.

The next day, one of my producers came to the studio and we all had a conference call with writer Jim Hart. Jim is an amazing writer. Some of his movie scripts include: Hook, Bram Stoker's Dracula, Mary Shelley's Frankenstein, Muppet Treasure Island, Contact, Lara Croft, Tomb Raider and The Cradle of Life. Jim agreed to help us write Snowyville. Jim took our script and worked on it for over a week. He made a few changes, but kept the core story. Jim was fond of the story. It reminded him of how he would set up his Christmas tree and village set with his daughter.

Brian, Andy, James and I took the "Snowyville" project to many financial investors that year. We met with several Wall Street Companies in August 2008. We were ready to make a deal with the Oppenheimer Film

Fund in New York City then the unthinkable happened.

Jim Hart and I traveled into New York City on September 28, 2008. The purpose of our trip was to talk over the financial terms of our upcoming deal. I should have been ecstatic. To think that our feature film was going to finally get financed was amazing. Jim and I met my sister, Francine, in New York City for dinner. We said our goodbyes. We were excited about our upcoming meeting the next day with Oppenheimer.

I was feeling a little uneasy because of several dreams I had the night before. I dreamt about my late father. He was in all my dreams and was warning me to be prepared for the worst. Then I thought maybe I was just nervous about getting ready to handle a feature film production.

The morning before our meeting, there was a 700 point drop in the Dow. It was September 29th, 2008. It was one of the largest point drops in the history of the New York Stock Exchange. That was the day the bailout bill failed in the Senate. It prompted widespread panic after the bankruptcy of Lehman Brothers.

Oppenheimer canceled our meeting and placed our project on permanent hold. This was a crushing blow for me and my team. Fortunately, Brian and Jim stayed optimistic. They still wanted to move forward with the project. The Jim Henson Studio became a production partner. We agreed to have Brian Henson produce the film as he championed me to be the director. I had the financial support of Pat Scire and Matt Phillips. The "Snowyville" script was polished. Continuing to move forward, we signed a term sheet contract with the Jim Henson Company in May 2009.

While I was in Hollywood, John Hadity called me. He wanted me to meet David Brookwell and Sean McNamara. David and Sean have produced some outstanding true-life story films that are well known today. They made the hit film *Soul Surfer*. It was based on a true story about a little girl who lost her arm to a shark attack while surfing in Hawaii. The movie was an acclaimed hit. It was also a commercial success. It put their production company on the map in Hollywood.

When I met David and Sean, I did not know what project I was going to shop to them. Sean was very interested in Once upon a Christmas Village, that was now named Snowyville. But, at the time, I wanted to keep that project open for Brian Henson and the Jim Henson Company. I decided on shopping him our live-action comedy film, Numba One.

This was in Living Magazine as a feature story

We obtained some seed money and drafted a few rewrites. We also agreed that Brookwell/McNamara would be the producers on the project. David Brookwell is a smart and crafty businessman. He truly understood the inner workings of Hollywood. He knew how to get projects funded and produced. David worked on a financial plan and we were ready to make a film. Having Sean McNamara direct the film was important to me because it was a comedy. Sean has a great sense of humor and I knew he was the right choice. I would work as a producer and a creative director. It was a perfect partnership.

We made the edits to the teaser and started to shop the film. Although we had many obstacles, we still made a lot of progress. We needed to secure investors, so we went to talk to Matt Phillips, Pat Scire, and Dr. Harry Bade. We raised $690,000. The funds were placed in our attorney's escrow account. What would happen next would change the course of my life and I never saw it coming.

We were getting ready to talk with a few more investors about completing our film fund. We then found out that our attorney had taken our money out of his escrow account and put it into a Ponzi scheme. He lost every cent. That attorney killed any hopes for our project. He also left us with very irate investors who wanted to know where their money went. Once again, a project was ready to go and derailed into the abyss. This was the end of a dream and the beginning of a nightmare for me and everyone who had supported me and the film.

Federico and I were desperate. We started trying to find ways to get more investors in. We needed to make the film and make good for the guys that had lost their investment. We raised a little bit of money through Michael Freedman. He did a promo short film piece for us to show the concept to investors. Little did we know, we had to wait until we settled with the attorney. Due to the attorney's ability to manipulate the system, this would take several years. The case finally came out of trial in New Jersey in 2016. The attorney agreed to settle his case and pay restitution for the money he lost plus attorney and court expenses. We are hoping that he makes good on the settlement and that one day we can still make the film. The person that stole our money was tracked down by the FBI. He was indicted and convicted in a ponzi scheme. Karma had the last laugh.

David and Sean still ask me how is that Mafia-comedy doing. I always respond with, "I can write a movie on how many ways you will get screwed if you're trying to make a Mafia movie!" David always gets a kick out of that. My goal now is for us to make a movie together, whether it is, Numba One, the Walt Disney Railroad Story or Snowyville. We have incredible scripts and wonderful production teams. Now all we need is the money and the right team to make them.

My personal attorney, Daniel Lavin, was amazing during this time. Daniel was trying to find a way to attract other investors to the projects. We met with several people that he thought would be interested. Unfortunately, we found ourselves having to wait until the litigation of Numba One was over. Daniel is a very smart attorney who knows entertainment law. He has kept me out of conflicts several times with people who were looking to scam us. I never liked attorneys until I met Daniel Lavin.

Now it was time to think about reinventing myself once again. One would think I was exhausted. I was! Mentally, physically and financially. I had to find ways to support my family and continue my passion for film making. Not an easy task when I was stuck in the middle of Orlando, Florida. The Mecca of theme park magic. Disney, Universal and Sea World. Just the thought of me having to start over was depressing. I had no idea how I was going to infiltrate Disney. I loved Disney. I grew up on Disney.

Getting on the Train to Disney World

With Lars Schilling in Southern Bavaria, Germany

I was with my family walking through EPCOT at Disney World. My children loved exploring the different countries. The German pavilion is one of our favorites since it the host of the outdoor train garden. I had a video camera and was videotaping our sons enjoying the train display. As I looked closer at the train display, I noticed that it was in great disrepair and needed an overhaul. Only one train engine was barely running. I didn't think that the trains met Disney show standards. I became inspired to help.

I had read a story, two weeks earlier, about the Marklin model train company. Marklin had recently purchased another outdoor train company named LGB. The Marklin Company has been making Germany made toys for over 150 years. The opportunity to pitch one of the greatest model train companies in the world, was too good to turn down.

I contacted Lars Schilling. He was the marketing director of Marklin/ LGB trains in Goppingen, Germany. Lars asked me to send over the video

I took of the train display at EPCOT. Lars promised to follow up and would see if they were interested in pursuing the project. I also sent him our original train designs for the "Snowyville Express."

A few weeks later, I received a call from Lars and Marklin. They flew me to Germany to work with them on several projects. One of the projects was to create the "Snowyville Express." The train engine and cars that I created were to be from my film "Snowyville." Lars made a prototype version of my design and the train model came out amazing. Lars flew to New Jersey to present the new prototype to Toys R Us.

I contacted Michael Berke and Mark Grill, who are seasoned toy sellers. They set up our Toys R Us meeting. They also agreed to represent our new train in the U.S. The buyer for Toys R Us saw the "Snowyville Express" train. She said, "I want that! That is amazing! Who designed it?" I replied, "My team designed it and Marklin will be producing the train."

We could have made the order with Toys R Us right then. However, we had many political issues with the Marklin's executive team. Lars tried to make the deal happen, but his CEO killed everything we brought to him. Later we found out that the CEO circumvented us. He made a deal directly with the Toys R Us buyer behind our backs with a different product line. It was a cheap China made train that Marklin and Toys R Us partnered on. It failed and it was a huge financial loss for both companies. I guess it was corporate business as usual. Once again, karma stepped in.

A few months later I arrived in Germany to meet Lars. We took the ICE (Inter City Expressway). Lars and the ride inspired me with new packaging and marketing ideas for the My World product line. Lars and I talked about many ideas on this train line. All our ideas were geared towards children. We thought of the kids who were just discovering the hobby of train collecting. We suggested to the Marklin executives that they could produce this line. It would be geared towards the Disney guest youth market. The new product line looked like the Disney Monorail and we were very excited. This would be perfect for the merchandising store at the German Pavilion in Disney's EPCOT.

Disney World would be a wonderful place to introduce our new product line of children's trains. During this time, it was also the beginning of the Apple iPad craze. That sparked another idea that I pitched to the Marklin executive team. I suggested that we put in a small camera, like the one on laptops, for internet chatting. The Marklin executive team thought I was crazy. Here I was thinking that they were innovators with creative visions. The only creative person in that room was Lars who understood my idea.

I continued to explain my idea. "If we put a little camera in the cab of the engine, people will be able to link it to their iPad with an APP that we create. Then they can see what a real train conductor would see if they were driving the train. Imagine, our buyers will be able to see inside their own personal train displays as if it was a real world in real time."

Lars and I both thought that this idea would separate us from every other train maker in the world. It would be on the cutting edge of technology. Unfortunately, the Marklin board of directors laughed at us. They said "that no one cares about that. We should stop wasting time on wasteful projects. The iPad is just a fad."

I called Michael Broggie and told him about my ideas for the "My World" train line. I told him that it could be used by Disney. Michael sent me his book entitled, "Walt Disney's Railroad Story." I read the book on the plane ride home from Germany. After reading his book it was clear that I needed to get the "My World" product line into Disney's EPCOT.

I called Michael when I returned home. He reminded me that Disney has a long history with trains. He felt that I should pursue a deal with Disney merchandising. He said, "Some of Walt Disney's "Nine old Men" owned trains and ran them in their backyards. In fact, Disney's artist, Ward Kimble's train was a full-size engine. He bought it from a sugar plantation in Hawaii that he named the Emma Nevada. There are so many stories about Ward, Frank, Ollie and Walt, that I could write a book about that subject. Michael's story made me think that a Marklin/Disney relationship could really happen.

Lars and I worked on a marketing plan to bring Marklin's ICE train set to Disney. I had no idea where I had to go, who I had to pitch, or who could make the decision to buy. I began by cold calling Disney Merchandising and got a meeting. I had no idea what I was doing, but I was having fun trying.

I brought the Marklin ICE box set into Disney Merchandising. The buyers fell in love with the set and agreed to sell it at the EPCOT German Pavilion Toy Store. The only stipulation was that I had to personally sell them in the store for three days a week. This was a dream come true for me. I made a wonderful business relationship between Marklin and Disney. I would represent the product on the EPCOT stage. In one month, we sold over 270 sets at $99.00 a set.

Our Train display at EPCOT German Pavilion Teddy Bear Store

We beat the Steiff Bear Company in sales and took over their space in the German Pavilion Toy Store. I was working with Disney Imagineering creating an experience that guests would love. Disney Imagineering commissioned me to create a diorama village with our train set. It would be fully operational and protected under a display case. It became a huge hit with the Disney guests. The children loved the interactive experience. We learned that a working train model sold more units than we ever imagined. We sold more train accessory sets, since people could see the train working. They also heard my presentation when I was onsite three days a week. I was selling and telling the story about Walt Disney and his love of trains.

Then Disney Imagineering came to talk to me. They wanted me to revamp the outdoor live train display at the German Pavilion. They were running older LGB trains and the train experience needed a facelift. I went to Germany to meet with Lars about placing new LGB trains in the train garden. We shipped back several boxes of new LGB train products. Then went to work on restoring the aesthetic look of the German landscape. It was a labor of love and a lot of fun. It allowed me to re-kick my creative juices and work with Disney Imagineering.

Me with Alice Davis, wife of the late Disney Legend Marc Davis

Later that month, I got a call from the lead Disney Imagineer on our project. He put me in touch with a TV producer who was producing a show called *My Yard Goes Disney*. The show was on HGTV and was very popular. They hired me to design and create an outdoor train display for one of their shows. It was a great success and the show aired with positive response. A few episodes later, the producers and the network had an argument and the show was canceled for good. They were having contract disputes. It was a shame because it was a great concept and we were planning bigger outdoor train designs for future shows.

Then the CEO of Marklin made one of the worst business decisions ever. He decided to try and circumvent my team and me and work directly with Disney merchandising. He failed to realize that we were the brand who was making the magic and selling the product at Disney. No one else could tell the story like us and sell units the way we did. It was all about marketing.

There were a few months of disputes between both companies. Lars resigned his position and Marklin stopped sending us train products. Lars and I could not believe that the CEO was making such a huge mistake. Lars resigned his position because of his CEO's unethical behavior. He had no confidence in his executive board. He fought for our deal and was not able to reach an agreement with the CEO and board for us to continue our business at Disney. I have so much respect and love for Lars because he stood by my side the whole time and we went down together. Not long after, Markiln's CEO was fired and the company was taken over by Sieber & Sohn. Karma, that girl's got my back.

My wife and I would no longer be selling our trains to Disney. It was a very sad day for me when I had to take down my train display in the German Toy Store at EPCOT. Several Disney guests complained, but the magic was over. We had a wonderful experience while it lasted! It was so unfortunate that it ended so soon. As for Lars? Lars went on to a better position in a new company that embraces his talent and visions. Lars and I are still working together and have a bright future ahead of us.

My Financial Crash was Real!

I worked for three years without a salary. We lived off our life savings. I had to make this right for my friends and family who invested in my dreams of making films. I believed that if you ask, then things will happen! I wasn't asking for the right things. I joined forces with my friend, George Lopez, who helped me start a small studio in Orlando. George is one of my most trusted friends and I respect his talents. We had a great concept but no money to make it successful.

I met Michael Freedman, a businessman from Connecticut in 2011. Michael and I decided to try and get some of my newer projects off the ground. We were working on a few animation ideas and attempting to reboot the live action Mob/romantic comedy, Numba One. Michael was like Matt Phillips and Pat Scire. These are great men who believed in my dreams and went out of their way to support me. They all believed in my ability to create and make film magic. But, we always fell short on raising enough capital to produce a product. Michael and I spent money on development and designs. We even tried to make a movie with college students who we thought were hungry. At first, we had 20 animators, but by month's end, it dwindled down to four. That's what happens when you ask for everyone to defer their salary until the movie gets sold.

I tried to make something positive happen for my animation business with Michael. Unfortunately, after a few years, I had to claim personal bankruptcy in 2012. It was one of the hardest decisions I ever had to make. I discovered that I was in good company.

Walt Disney, Mark Twain, Ulysses S. Grant, Abraham Lincoln, Rembrandt, Thomas Paine, Henry Ford, Milton Hershey, Oscar Wilde, P. T. Barnum, Dorothy Hamill, Kim Bassinger, Larry King and Elton John are only a few people that also went bankrupt in their careers.

They all bounced back and created better financial success when they recovered. I'm not proud of filing for bankruptcy. In fact, it was one of the hardest things I ever had to do. I was so depressed that I remember telling my wife that I was in the loser Hall of Fame. Never did I think that I would ever have financial issues. I was always the one hustling to make a fair dollar. I worked every job possible to make a buck and I was not afraid to start over. This was a challenging time for me and my growth as a father and husband. I never wanted my core family to feel the pain I was experiencing. I tried to make life as normal as I could make it for them. I sold a few of my assets that year to help keep our lifestyle going, but it was tough to keep up with the Joneses.

I even lost my Range Rover baby. No worries. It's just a car.

We lost everything! We lost our Range Rover, our house in New Jersey in a short sale, our stocks, my grandfather's coin collection and several other huge material assets. I made it before and I'll make it again!

At the end of the day, they were all material things. Material things-that's all it was! Things that I have asked for in the past and received them. I had faith that I would be able to ask the universe for those things once more and receive them. I was the richest man alive and I didn't even know it at the time. I had my health, my wife, my sons, my family and friends. My mother and two sisters supported me when I fell. I owe so much to them. Never did our friend know or our children feel the pressure.

It's not about how we fall, it's all about how we can get up. I have never worked as hard as I have in the past several years to make up for my losses. I believe that a good fall will teach you how to become more humble, spiritual and respectful of humanity. I will never regret the path I chose and I never will blame someone else for my own mistakes. I made decisions and I must live with them.

I have done my best philanthropic work, even though I did not have a pot to piss in. I appreciated the lessons I learned more from my failures than I have ever learned from my successes. This was how it happened and I embraced it as the will of God. I grew as a man, a father and a husband. I can't stress enough how important that fall was for me to grow as a better human-being for mankind. Today, I can stop and smell the roses. As Dr. Seuss said, "Don't be sad that it's over. Be happy that it happened."

I've been told that "It's always darkest before the dawn." It was Thanksgiving week in 2012. We had just lost our dog due to a freak accident at the Veterinarian's office. On the way going to Fort Lauderdale, the normal mood of happiness turned bleak and hopeless. Our children were crying and Daddy had no way to comfort them until we got to our destination. My in-laws had a time-share in Fort Lauderdale and we had been spending Thanksgiving there for several years. Colleen and I thought it might be good to get away with the family for a few days after that tragic news about our dog. It was the right move since everyone was busy, keeping them distracted. A few days later, Colleen and I were talking about how to get back on the financial trail. Instead of making my bank account grow, I was blessed by making my family grow. Colleen had news that we would be expecting our third child. We went from being completely devastated to totally overjoyed. It's funny how life takes you on a roller coaster ride. Matthew was born on July 23, 2013. Once again I became the richest man in the world!

A Great Idea Never Gets Old

Cover page of Florida Sporting News 50th issue.

I knew that with the economy trying to rebound, I needed to create a way to help promote my community. That is when I reached back into my bag of memories. I pulled out the idea that propelled me during my first rise to financial independence. The same sports paper I had started 22 years ago in New Jersey was calling to me once again in Orlando.

I started the Florida Sporting News in spring of 2014. I went around Orlando selling advertising. I was collecting the local sports news from local Orlando high schools. My paper was a huge hit and is still going strong. It was amazing to me that there was not a sports publication here in the holy grail of high school sports.

Then one day, I met with a local athletic director of a major high school sports factory in Orlando. I'm not kidding, this school produces the most NFL and MLB players than any other school in the country. During our first meeting, I explained in detail what our paper would do for his school. I told him that we will only promote positive sports coverage for his athletic program.

The athletic-director looked at me and said "What are you going to do for me? How much money can you raise for me?" At first, I thought he was joking, but his eyes never left mine. He was serious! I looked right back into his eyes and said "Let's see what we can do. What kind of money do you need?"

"I need a new synthetic football field around 350 thousand dollars." he replied. I was learning that every high school must compete for advertising dollars. That is why a sports publication was never started in this area. The sports programs are incredible and the local following is huge. But, any business that wants to go into business with the schools needs to have deep pockets to share the wealth. I left that meeting fully understanding that I was not in New Jersey anymore! There's no place like home. There's no place like home. I clicked my sneakers but nothing happened.

I had to structure my new business to include an existing partner that I never knew I was going to have. One for me, two and three for them. I work harder and smarter than I ever had to. Currently, the paper is in all 30 public and private schools in Orange County.

These people put our community before the almighty dollar. They understand what we needed to do for our local athletes. Social media was taking over our children. Sports help to keep the kids out of trouble and helps them stay focused. Sports are very important to our community. Our online website and Facebook sites are expanding with more traffic every month.

If it weren't for partners like Carlos Sciortino, Alan Schneider, Sunil Prakash, Raul Ceide, Windermere Prep, Kim Praniewicz, Kim Carroll, Grayson Everidge, Bob Gall and George Lopez, our publication would have never survived.

THE NFL ALUMNI

While visiting my family in New Jersey, I received a call from my old NFL buddy, Bart Oats. Bart was with the Super Bowl Giants. He asked me if I wanted to play in the New Jersey NFL Alumni Golf Tournament in North Jersey. I agreed and went up to play.

With Ron Jaworski and Hall of Fame inductees Kellen Winslow Sr. and Jack Youngblood at an NFL groundbreaking event

At the event, I met with Joe Pisarcik. I had known Joe for many years from playing in the Ron Jawarski's Golf outing in Atlantic City. Joe was the new CEO/President of the NFL Alumni. We had a nice conversation and I convinced him to meet with me about starting a new NFL Alumni chapter in Florida. We met at Rod's Tavern in Spring Lake, New Jersey. It was down the street from where Bill Parcells lived. The same house where I had dropped a letter in mail slot years before.

I felt it was necessary to push the issue to start a new chapter in Orlando to Joe. I knew there were many former NFL players who lived here and were not being represented. I also knew that is was an opportunity to use the shield to help raise money for local charities here in Orlando. I had a lot of support from local businesses and former NFL players.

Pisarcik and I had a two-hour meeting. He was impressed that I had a drive and passion for helping children. The Caring for Kid's mission has been in my blood for many years. I was a member of the NFL Alumni since 1993. Joe knew my commitment to the NFL Alumni and the mission of "Caring for Kids."

Larry Little and me on Fox Sports during the Super Bowl

After our meeting, Joe awarded an NFL Alumni Central Florida Chapter to be set up. We were approved. We now could contact former NFL players in the central Florida area for recruitment. We were the first and only chapter at the time, which did not have a hosted NFL team in its city. Our chapter started swinging right out of the gate. The CFO at the time was Elvis Gooden Sr. Elvis championed the idea of a new chapter and became my mentor. His support was the catalyst for why I was awarded the chapter. Elvis helped to start a successful chapter. He advised me on how to navigate through the shark infested waters of NFL politics.

If you ever wanted a great chess player on your team, Elvis is the man.

In October 2014, my fellow NFL players voted me in as chapter President. Seneca McMillan was our Vice-President. We worked hard that first year trying to recruit local businesses and former NFL players. Our chapter raised over $100,000.00 in money and trade for several local children's charities in Orlando. One of my favorite charities is One Heart for Women and Children. It was founded by Stephanie Bowman, who is an incredible person. Her charity does so much good work for women and children in Orlando, Florida.

It was an honor to help Stephanie feed so many people in need. She has inspired me to be a philanthropist. The children we helped have taught me how to love humanity. I learned the sense of caring, nourishing, developing, and enhancing what it means to be human. That is the most rewarding gift from God that he has shared with us all.

That same year, I met Hall of Fame golfer Chi-Chi Rodriguez at the NFL Alumni golf tournament in Naples, Florida. We came up to a Par 3 on the course and Chi-Chi was there challenging golfers for $20 for whoever can get the closest to the pin. All the guys took a chance with $20 in hopes to beat Chi-Chi and win $50 in the Golf Pro Shop. They all lost the challenge.

When it was my turn, I asked Chi-Chi if he would shoot first. He replied, no! You go first! I replied, "I'll put up $40 if you go first and I'll buy you a beer and a cigar." Without skipping a beat, Chi-Chi said "The beers and cigars are free and after what Monica Lewinsky did with her cigar with Clinton, I think I'll pass on the cigar." The guys all laughed and Chi-Chi accepted my challenge. Chi-Chi Rodriguez hit the ball with beauty and finesse, and his ball landed three feet away from the pin.

My friends were counting it as a loss for me and were saying that I should just pay him now. I took a deep breath and kept my head down. I had nothing to lose. I was going up against a Hall of Fame golfer. That's not too much pressure.

I used a nice easy nine iron. The ball landed two feet away from the pin and the guys went crazy as they tackled me to the ground. Chi-Chi walked over and shook my hand like the gentleman he is. That is my only claim to fame against a PGA golfer. I beat Chi-Chi Rodriguez for the closest to the pin contest. Chi Chi is one of the most sincere human beings that I know. The positive work he does for all the children of the world makes a huge difference in their lives. I've seen this man work and talk to children on their level, never making them feel like they were beneath him. He's a quality person who will leave an incredible Legacy.

After starting a new NFL Alumni chapter from scratch and spending

With Hall of Fame Golfer Chi-Chi Rodriguez

With Hall of Fame inductee and my great friend Larry Little

two years of dedicated service, I decided to step down as President and spend more time with my sons, write this book and make a movie.

During my time as President, I met some great guys, who inspired me and made an impression on my life. I am proud to call them my friends.

With Larry and Conner Heath of Tommy Bahama at an NFL event

One incredible former NFL football player is Larry Little. He will always have a special place in my heart. He is a Hall of Fame inductee and a former Miami Dolphins player of the 17-0 undefeated team.

Larry is not little at all. He has one of the largest hearts I know. He's a wonderful husband, an incredible father and grandfather. But most of all, he has a pure heart and is always willing to help his friends and people he has never met. He reminds me quite a lot of my other HOF friend, Michael Strahan. They both are two great guys. They treat everyone with respect.

Another man I met on my journey was Coach Lou Holtz. I have had the privilege to listen to several of Coach Holtz's speeches and presentations. Having the honor to be involved with football all my life, I've had many opportunities to be inspired by leaders of men. Coach Holtz is the pinnacle of inspiration and motivation. Coach has a way to reach inside a player's heart and strike those chords of courage. I have had the unique opportunity to play golf with him. If you ever want to learn more about yourself and be a better human being, play golf with Coach Lou Holtz. That was some of the greatest hours I have ever spent on a golf course. His stories were captivating and exciting.

Coach Lou Holtz lives in Lake Nona, Florida. We have been in several golf outings together. When Coach walks into a room every eye is on him. Lou is one of the humblest people I know. He's very intelligent and is careful with his words. I have learned so much when I listen to him.

Lou is a leader of great men. He is a great golfer and a highly respected Coach.

With Coach Lou Holtz at an Orlando charity event for children

With HOF friends Ted Hendricks and Larry Little

The NFL Calls - Now I'm on the Other Side

With Tony, John and Alan at the Miami Dolphins scrimmage

In 2013, I received a call from an old pal and former NFL player Keith Elias. Keith told me that the NFL started a new program called the NFL Legends Community. They invited 100 former NFL players to attend a transitional program called T.A.P. I decided to go. I dragged one of my NFL buddies Seneca McMillan, to experience this program with me. We did not know what to expect, but it sounded exciting to us. We worked with life coaches, spiritual leaders and educators at Georgia Tech University. When we finished the four, 12-hour days, we received a business degree from Georgia Tech University

On the drive home from Georgia, I decided that I had a higher purpose. I wanted to help all my NFL brothers who did not attend this opportunity. My idea was to bring the NFL's T.A.P program to Orlando. We had already started the NFL Alumni chapter in Orlando. My mission was to inform and assist the NFL teammates in my area. I could teach them how to network with local business owners. I didn't know how I was going to do it. I just did it!

While I was at the TAP program, I met Terell Canton from the NFL Officiating Department. Terell was recruiting former players into a new NFL officiating program. Seneca and I were interested in the program.

We had to take a few tests before we signed up. We were hoping to be candidates for the upcoming season. Later in 2014, we both received a call from the NFL officiating department.

They started a new program called LODP. It was fast tracking former NFL players to become football officials. I trained with NFL and NCAA officials at the Tom Beard's camp in Maryland. I was invited to start officiating with the CFOA (Central Florida Officiating Association). Mitch Fazzio was the VP of football operations for the CFOA and I asked to meet with him. Mitch and I met at a burger place in Lake Mary, Florida.

I told Mitch, "I want to be a football official." Mitch looked at me and said, "OK, what do you know about officiating football?" I replied, "I officiated in New Jersey for two years as a field judge, but that was 24 years ago." Mitch looked at me with a surprised look. Then he said, "And you want to get back into officiating football now at your age?" I nodded my head yes. Mitch continued, "Ok, that's a tall order but I'll try." We laughed.

A week later, I had a meeting with Roy Ellison. He is currently working as an NFL official. He lives in my hometown of Windermere, Florida. Roy looked at me and said, "You want to be a field judge? No! You're an umpire. You look the part of an umpire. You could get away with being an umpire. You're overweight and you look slow. You would make for a great high school umpire." Roy was right. I was 45 pounds overweight. I needed to get my health in order before I could think about running around with younger kids who have incredible speed. I lost 45 pounds in 8 months and was running to the gym three times a week.

That season, I worked as a football umpire for "Friday Night Lights" high school varsity football games in Orange County. I did Junior Varsity games on Thursdays and Pop Warner games on Saturdays. In the summer of 2015, the NFL sent me to work with an NFL crew at the Miami Dolphins summer training camp. I had gotten myself into the best shape of my life.

When I arrived at Coral Gables, Florida I checked into the Radisson Hotel. I went into my hotel room and there was a huge NFL bag on the bed. In the bag were NFL shirts, hats and other Miami Dolphins logo items. It reminded me of the first day of my NFL camp with the L.A. Raiders.

There were several gift baskets there waiting for me to open sent by a few friends. I took a deep breath and looked up to heaven and said, "Thank you God!" I sat there on my hotel floor and cried for a good 10 minutes. All I could think about was, 'If my father could see me now, what would he have said?" My father respected football officials. I was also thinking about the financial challenges I had to endure and how I was now starting on the rise once again.

I met with Tony Michalek, an incredible NFL official, at a local restaurant. During our conversation, we got to know each other much better. Tony is a straight up, to the point guy, who will never sugar coat a conversation. Tony is my kind of man! We talked about my professional career with the NFL and what I was currently doing. Our conversation was real and very constructive. I don't ever remember having such an honest and caring conversation with others in the NFL.

I met with the rest of the crew that night during a dinner. The crew included: NFL legend official Jerry Markbreit, John Hussey-first year NFL

With Alan Baynes, Tony Michalek, Jerry Markbreit and Jon Hussy

referee, Alan Baynes and Tony Michalek. I was the fly on the wall that night. I said very little and just listened to NFL greatness. I was humble to be with these men.

The next morning, I woke up early and met Jerry Markbreit in the hotel lobby. Out of nowhere, NFL Quarter Back football legend, Joe Theisman walked up to us and said hello to Jerry. Joe looked at me and said "I know you. You're with the NFL Alumni, right?" I replied, "Yes, I'm Mike Attardi and we've met a few times over the years at NFL events."

I had my cell phone in my hand. I knew that this was a great opportunity to take a photo with Joe, since he was my mother's favorite NFL player. Jerry took the photo and I made my mother very happy when I sent it to her. She was mad that I didn't take a photo with Joe the last time we were together. I made some points with Mom.

With Joe Theisman

Later, I was at an official's meeting at the Dolphin's facility and Dan Marino walked into our meeting. It was nice to know that he still remembered me from back in my playing days. Dan and I had spent a few days together in Tokyo, Japan, during the American Bowl in 1991. We had a lot of fun together as we got to know and understand that complex culture.

I have a long history with the Dolphin organization

Then Colleen called and told me that our younger son, Matty had a high fever. After her phone call, Colleen and I decided we needed to keep in contact while I was in Miami. I was at an offensive meeting with the Dolphins. Tony was speaking to the guys about the new NFL official rules.

With Dan Marino and sister-in-Law Monica

I thought I had shut off my phone, but it started to ring. My ring tone was the song "*Bad to the Bone.*" I was scrambling through my bag to find it. I looked like a rabid raccoon trying to get a piece of food. All the guys started to laugh and said, "That's a $500 fine bro!" Tony looked at me with disgust. When I tried to explain, what had happened, he was very calm, but I saw the NFL official come out in him. He explained the rule to me about why I was going to be charged for the foul. I was charged a foul. Then I was hazed by the crew when they learned about what had happened.

That same morning, I had taken medicine for my allergies. The hotel I was staying in had dust mites in the room and I am highly allergic to dust mites. Later we went into a special team meeting where I fell asleep because of the medicine and the dark room. My crew took a photo of me which showed me as an "Official caught sleeping during a Dolphin's meeting." We had a few laughs about it until I found out that the picture had made the NFL Officials wire! I never lived that one down. Then it was reported to my boss in New York. I had a lot of explaining to do. My crew also made me the designated driver that night for a dinner in Fort Lauderdale as my punishment.

The next day was a pre-season game preparation. I learned a great deal of information as we worked on game mechanics and rules. I discovered that the details of game day preparations are hard work.

That night, we drove to South Florida University and got dressed in our uniforms for the game. I went to the bathroom several times. My stomach was turning upside down with excitement. And, just before the game I was told that I would be the head linesman.

I was nervous because my preferred position was an umpire, not a linesman. I was playing out my position on every future play. I was never so focused on what I needed to do. In fact, I was so focused that I forgot about being scared.

As the game progressed, John Hussey our referee, kept looking over at me. At first, I thought I was doing something wrong. Later I learned, that Tony asked John to put me in at the umpire position for the last two minutes of the game. That means that the NFL Umpire moves back to his original position, which is behind the linebackers on defense.

I was put in as an umpire during the Miami Dolphins scrimmage game. John Hussey walked over to me and calmly said, "Do not throw a flag, Attardi." John knew I was scared out of my mind. We had a great laugh afterwards about his good advice.

There were great moments that I got out of that Miami Dolphins camp. I met my mentor and friend, Tony Michalek. Tony is a seasoned NFL official that took me under his wing. I thank God for connecting us. He's a great friend.

Tony and I had an in-depth conversation about the strong commitment it takes to be an NFL official. It's also about 'who you know' in the NFL to help get you advanced. I took Tony's advice and worked even harder that high school football season. I worked 127 games that season.

Then I was invited to try-out for the NAIA Sun Conference in Florida. I made the Sun Conference and started as an umpire in the fall of 2016. I also picked up several University of Florida practices from my other mentor and friend, Wally Hough. I met Wally during a football officiating camp when he was my instructor and we've been good friends ever since.

In the spring of 2017, I worked five University of Florida Gator practices and scrimmages with Wally Hough, one University of Miami scrimmage with Deon Lawrence and Tra Blake and two University of Central Florida scrimmages with Chris Brown and NFL Umpire Roy Ellison. Not bad by anyone's standards.

During the summer of 2017, I was hired to work with the University of Miami as a practice and scrimmage umpire. In fall of 2017, I worked over 20 scrimmages and got to know and respect the coaches and players for the Miami Hurricanes.

Meeting Roy Patrick Disney

I had meetings with The Carolwood Society at Walt Disney World. I had the honor and privilege to take a private tour of the Magic Kingdom. I had lunch with Roy Patrick Disney. He's the grandson of the famous Roy O. Disney. Roy is Walt Disney's brother and lifelong business partner. He helped build Walt Disney World.

Michael & Sharon Broggie, Roy Patrick Disney at Disney World

Roy is a fascinating man. He was very open to share many of the Disney family stories with me. Roy was proud of his grandfather's and Great Uncle Walt's accomplished in life. Their accomplishments live on for future generations to enjoy.

One story that he shared was very endearing about Walt Disney. It showed how much Walt Disney tried to live a normal life. The story was about Diane Disney, (Walt's Daughter), and takes place on her first day of school in second grade. A teacher asked if she was Diane Disney. Diane, who was only seven years old, replied, "No, I'm Diane." The teacher insisted that Diane's last name was Disney and that her father owned Disneyland. Diane adamantly disagreed with the teacher and said that her father worked on movies.

When Diane came home from school, she marched into the living room. Her father was in his easy chair, reading a newspaper. Diane walked in and pulled the paper down. She asked her father, "Are you Walt Disney?" Walt replied, "Honey, I'm daddy." Then he raised his paper and continued to read. Diane pulled the paper down once more and again asked. "Are you Walt Disney?" Walt looked in her eyes. Then he said, "It's a little complicated, honey, but yes, when I'm home I'm daddy, but when I'm at work I am Walt Disney.

Walt raised the paper again to read. Diane pulled the paper down again. She put her hands on her hips and looked angry as she stated, "You never told me you were Walt Disney!" Walt and Lillian had a good laugh over that one. That simple story makes me a bigger fan of the man behind the Mouse, the Theme Parks and Walt Disney's lifelong legacy.

Michael and Sharon Broggie with Roy Patrick Disney at Disney World

Roy was gracious to have lunch with me, Michael and Sharon Broggie. We spoke about the past, but also about some of the dreams and passions he still has for the Disney Company today. Roy's ideas were magical and heartfelt. I heard the genuine passion in his voice, which was very exciting to me.

He knew I was working with the Monorail, so he began a conversation about a possible Monorail expansion. We looked at how the parks would benefit from this bold move. We agreed that a newer and much more advanced Monorail system was needed. It would make for a better guest relations experience for all Disney's guests.

We also spoke in detail about making the guest experiences better. We could take the lead through media technology. It was almost like being with Walt and listening to his new ideas and concepts before he was THE Walt Disney. Roy had so much passion when he was talking about his family's legacy. One must wonder, why isn't Roy Patrick Disney on the Disney Board of Directors? To have a Disney family member back with the company would most likely drive up the Disney stock price. I was honored to get the opportunity to meet with someone I never imagined I'd have to pleasure of meeting.

Bob Gurr, me, Stephanie Bowmen, and Michael Broggie.

I had the honor to spend quality time with Disney Legend Bob Gurr. Bob was one of the first Disney Imagineers that worked directly with Walt Disney.

Robert "Bob" Gurr (born October 25, 1931) is an Imagineer and Disney Legend responsible for designing most, if not all, of the ride vehicles for many early Disneyland attractions. Disney insiders often refer to these as "Gurrmobiles".

Gurr was first hired by W.E.D. Enterprises, better known today as Walt Disney Imagineering. Among the many projects Gurr developed and designed are the Autopia vehicles, the Flying Saucers, the antique cars and double decker buses on Disneyland's Main Street, the Haunted

Mansion Doom Buggies, the Disneyland Monorail, The Submarine Voyage, and the Matterhorn Bobsleds. Gurr also helped design the inner mechanics of Disney's first Audio-Animatronics figure, Abraham Lincoln, used in Great Moments with Mr. Lincoln. That's not bad for anyone's standards.

With Disney Legend Bob Gurr

Michael Broggie and I were having our monthly phone call and something Michael said lit the light bulb in my brain. I suggested that we try and get Bob and him down to Walt Disney World to talk to our Disney Transportation Cast members. Michael thought it was a great idea. Once again, I had no idea how I was going to do it. I approached management at Disney and they thought it would be an honor to have both Bob Gurr and Michael Broggie talk to our cast members. They also felt that bringing in Disney legends would help inspire and educate as well.

The August 2017 event was a smash hit with over 200 cast members in attendance. Not only did the Disney Cast have a chance to learn from these legends but they were able to meet and greet with them afterwards. Bob and Michael stayed until every photo and autograph was signed. A true testament to their love for Walt Disney and the brand he created. Michael has said, "Everyone who works at any Disney theme park has a huge responsibility. Our Cast members are walking where Walt Disney did or would have, if he was still alive. We continue where he left off and we now have that torch to pass onto future generations. Our actions are louder than words."

I have so many stories to share about Bob and Michael. One of my favorites is the time that Bob had just finished making the prototype car for the Autopia ride. They needed a young test driver and Walt suggested Michael at the age of 12 to be that driver. The Disney Company documented the young Michael Broggie driving around the backlot of the Disney Animation Studios. When Michael tells the story in front of Bob, Bob always cuts him off in mid-sentence. Bob says, "Oh come on Michael, you weren't the test driver for the Autopia car. You were the test dummy!" Michael responded, "My dad really never liked you anyway." Both of them laugh. Michael's father was Roger Broggie who was Bob's boss at Disney in the 1950's and they were very close friends.

I agree with Michael. As a Disney Cast member, we have the responsibility to walk in Walt's footsteps. When I was seven years old, I watched the Monorail come through the Contemporary Resort. It was one of the most exciting things I saw during my younger years. I turned to my father and said, "Someday I'm gonna drive the Monorail Dad." My father smiled and said, "You are able to do anything you want if you work hard. First, I want you to go to college and then maybe you can retire and drive the Monorail." Once again, if you dream it, it will happen with hard work.

Golf is my Sanctuary

"My worst day in golf will surpass my best day at work!"

Golf has always served as my sanctuary when I needed to clear my mind. For some people, golf is stressful. For me, golf is a way of life. It's the only game in the world where you can get to know the person you're playing with, since you have four hours together. I have made some of my best business deals on a golf course.

I've learned that people who cheat in golf will cheat in life. I have also learned that the people who play it where it lies, are the most honest people I know. If you want to learn more about a person, take them golfing. Their true personality will come out. I could write a book about all the crazy stories I've experienced during golf.

Some are funny and some are plain sad. I've seen grown men cry, throw their clubs, and even take their whole bag with clubs and throw them into a pond. Then, later they realized that their car keys and wallet were in their bag! I have been blessed playing golf. My friends know me as a serious but fun golfer who loves the game. I'm competitive but fair and I like to win. It's in my DNA.

For the record, I'm sharing these accomplishments in a humble way, I have won three NFL Players Association Golf tournaments (Atlanta,

1998, New Orleans, 1998 and New Jersey, 1999). I came in second three times (Hawaii, 2001, Hawaii 2007 and Orlando 2016), and won three NFL Alumni Golf Tournaments (New York, 2001, New Jersey 2002 and Orlando 2015).

The PGA has recorded 18 holes in one for me starting with my first ACE in 1997 to my recent ACE in 2016 at The Slammer & Squire of the Hall of Fame of Golf in St. Augustine, Florida. (Thank God, I had witnesses for all 18) In 2013, I placed in four PGAM and section events. My biggest wins were the Waldolf Astoria and Ritz-Carlton invitational. I was also a member of the winning team for the Florida State Rider Cup over the FAGCJ in 2013.

In St. Augustine, FL at the Hall of Fame of Golf where I have several bricks to showcase my hole-in ones. With my sons Matthew, Michael Jr., Nathaniel and my father-in-law Richard "Dick" Cole-Hatchard in 2015.

I have won 22 amateur golf tournaments from 1999 thru 2016. I currently play in the Florida PGAM, an amateur golf league representing the Orlando section. As you can see, I really love to play golf. I hope I can inspire my sons to someday take up the game.

One of my favorite, golf stories happened while I was with my brother-in-law, Carl Nordell. We were playing golf in South Carolina and we were both shooting a great score. We came to a par 4 and both of us were one under par after twelve holes. Carl had a massive drive and his second shot landed only a few feet from the green. I knew that I had to go for the green and not lay-up since Carl was making every putt that day. I was 225 yards out and I pulled out my three wood. I had a slight wind in my face but decided to go for it anyway. I didn't care about the large lake as much as the sand bunkers that surrounded the green.

I took a deep breath and hit my Titleist ball with much authority and finesse. I was thinking that this was going to be one of my greatest golf shots. My ball was heading straight for the green. Then a fear of doubt hit me when a gust of wind waved past my pants. I start talking to the ball as if it was able to hear my plea, "Come on baby, make it! Come on." Splash! My Titleist number 4 ball was now a fish toy. I said, "I know I can make this shot. I'll take a drop right here." Carl shook his head, "You can take a drop at the point where it entered the pond. That's around a hundred yards closer." Before he finished speaking, I had already dropped another Titleist ball at the same spot. I responded, "I will make this shot."

Once again, I hit an amazing shot and once again my ball found the water. I took out another ball and dropped it again. Like the other two balls, I was donating more Titleist for the fish to play with. Carl was shaking his head in disbelief and reminded me that I did not have to drop from this distance. At one point, he started to laugh and called me "Tin Cup." The reference to a golf movie with Kevin Costner. Carl said, "Give it up, you can't make it from here."

At that point, it was not about the score. It was about showing Carl that I could do it and it was about challenging myself to make the shot. This was my fourth attempt and I had to make it over. I dropped my Titleist number 2 ball and took a deep breath. I pulled back my club and swung with all my might. I felt like time was standing still, although it was only a few seconds before the ball landed on the green. I was only six feet away from the pin. I smiled.

Carl said, "Well, if you make the putt that would be the greatest eleven I've ever seen." Carl was right. I should have dropped the ball a hundred-yards closer with my third ball. I should've left that hell of a hole with a possible six. I said to Carl, "If I took the drop where I should have taken it then we wouldn't have such a great story to tell our kids one day." Carl smiled and nodded his head in agreement.

That is the game of golf. Somedays every shot is perfect and it makes you want to come back again. Then somedays you can't hit the side of a barn and it makes you want to come back even more. My definition of a perfect golf day is finishing the round with the same ball you started with. It's also being with people you love and learning how to get better at this crazy game called golf.

My son Nathaniel and I at the PGA Hall of Fame pointing too my two "hole in one" bricks.

A Scouting Life for Me

With my sons, Nathaniel and Michael Jr. in Washington, DC. Mikey received a Congressional Award and was presented the Medal of Merit by the Boy Scouts

I became a fan of the Boys Scouts of America when I was ten years old. I belonged to a Cub Scout Pack located at Elberon Elementary School. I achieved the rank of Arrow of Light and was on my way into Boy Scouts. However, I quit before I got there. I told them I stopped scouting because my father thought it was a gateway into the Armed Forces. He didn't want me to follow his path into the military. The real reason was because I could not make the scout sign with my fingers. That is true, my hand did not have the dexterity to hold up my three fingers together. I was very embarrassed, so I stopped Boy Scouts after my Arrow of Light rank. That was my loss and I always said that if I ever had sons, I would like them to join scouting.

With full respect for my father, he was right. I wanted to be like him and did think the military sounded like fun. In fact, years later, when the movie Top Gun came out in the theaters, I wanted to quit college and be a fighter pilot. That was a short-lived dream once my father found out that I had the crazy idea to enlist during Desert Storm. My father rarely yelled at me, but when he did, I listened.

My father was a little overprotective of me. But if you know anything about scouting, it does prepare you for life. I regretted it years later when I saw some of my fellow scouting friends achieving the rank of

Eagle. I believe the rank of an Eagle Scout is a shoe-in for college. I say this because all my friends that were scouts were accepted into big time colleges. Think about it, a college recruiter looks at a student that was not in scouting as average. A student that has similar scores, but is also an Eagle Scout has an advantage. To achieve the rank of an Eagle Scout, you need to be dedicated, persistent and determined. A college recruiter sees the Eagle Scout as a better investment. They see that an Eagle Scout will most likely stay in school and try to achieve the hardest task assigned to him.

When my son Mikey turned nine years old, Colleen and I got him into Cub Scouts. Mikey loved it so much that I volunteered as a Cub Scout Tiger Leader for my other son, Nathaniel. I served for seven years as a den leader for Pack 223 and an (ASM) Assistant Scoutmaster for troop 225, both located in Windemere. Florida. One of the most rewarding things that I can do as an adult leader, is to help young boys become independent young men.

Scouting teaches teamwork, honesty, bravery and how to be self-reliant. It's also a great way to get my sons out of the house, where they can get consumed playing video games. I forced them to go outside and explore, so they could be one with nature in the great outdoors.

With Todd Chase and Chip Vanture at Wood Badge beading- 2017

During my own personal journey in Boy Scouts, I had the opportunity to help and lead many young men on their mission to reach the rank of Eagle Scout. I've had the honor and privilege to work with some incredible men in my community, who volunteer their time to help the local scouts. One day, Todd Chase, a friend of mine and fellow ASM, and I decided to take a step towards the highest honor given to an Assistant Scoutmaster in Boy Scouts called Wood Badge. The Wood Badge program is a very intense and exciting program. Not only do you attend two long weekend campouts, but once you complete the basics of Wood Badge, you must complete five tickets. What are tickets?

Tickets are chosen projects that you need to complete with either a Cub Scout or a Boy Scout Troop. My personal tickets dealt with diversity, teaching, leadership, skills building and charity. You only have 18 months to do all five tickets. You may think that's a long time, but it's not. Most of us have busy schedules and extra activities with your family. It can become very difficult at times.

Most people that start their tickets, never get a chance to complete them. Todd and I completed all five tickets in less than eleven months. Most of my tickets revolved around charitable contributions, which helped me achieve my goal.

Todd Chase and I were awarded our Wood Badge beads in January of 2017. It was awesome having the opportunity to share that experience with my friend Todd and Troop 225. We still talk about the fond memories we shared during those two hard cold weekends of camping. I logged in over 200 hours of community service. I was awarded the Silver Presidential Volunteer Service Award by President Barack Obama. In October 2017, I was awarded the Gold Presidential Volnteer Service Award by President Donald Trump.

I am currently serving my 8th year in scouting. It doesn't look like my adventures with them will end anytime soon. My son Nathaniel crossed over into Boy Scouts. My son, Mikey, is going for his Eagle rank. Our third son, Matthew, is only 4 years old and has one more year before he can join Cub Scouting. I can't complain, I cherish the time I have with my sons. Especially when we are out camping and I can teach them survival skills and share a story around the camp fire.

One of my fondest memories of scouting was when Mikey and I were at Skymont Campsite in the Tennessee Mountains. I was one of the ASM's with our troop and was so busy getting scouts to their classes all week that I never had a chance to see Mikey, aside from dinner time every night. We finally got our chance to spend some time one night when I found him walking back to camp.

With my son, Mikey at Skymont Camp in Tennessee and My three sons - Matthew, Mikey and Nate

It was a Friday and he had finished all his requirements for several Merit Badges. I told him to follow me. We took a two-mile hike to a location that another ASM told me to see, before we left because the view was incredible. After Mikey and I crossed two streams, did some rigorous rock climbing and hiked two miles over tough terrain, we found ourselves at the pinnacle of the mountain. It was the most unbelievable sight both of us had ever seen. We sat together on a large boulder and talked about life. It was the first time that Mikey and I had a real man to man type of conversation. Those are the memories I'll never forget.

The NFL Pro Bowl and Roger Goodell

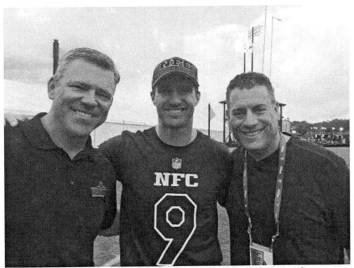

With Mark Brunell and Drew Brees at Pro Bowl practice

After we got home, we heard that the NFL Pro-Bowl was coming to Orlando on January 29, 2017. It would be the first time in the NFL history that the game would be played in Orlando. Every season, this game had always been played in Hawaii. It was not a very successful event for the NFL. In fact, they had talked about shutting the game down due to poor attendance and very poor TV ratings.

Eventually, the NFL decided to make a change. They announced that the Pro-Bowl was going to be awarded to Orlando. No one knew how to react. Not only did the NFL come in with kid gloves on, but the City of Orlando did not know how they were going to pull this off on time. The former players embraced the event and set up several NFL Alumni parties that would support the game and also the legend players that made the game of football what it is today.

The NFL was coming to Orlando. So was my old friend and place-kicking holder, Coach Jason Garrett of the Dallas Cowboys. He was the Head Coach for the NFC team. If you remember, Coach Garrett and I go way back to my high school/college years when I used to go over to the Garrett's house to practice football at the age of 16.

With Dez Bryant and Dax Prescott of the Dallas Cowboys

I had not seen Jason for several years but when we connected at the practice, it was like no time had passed between us. We picked-up our friendship like we did a few years earlier. That is when you know you have a great friend. No matter how successful he is now in the NFL, he would never make his friends feel like they were beneath him. We had a wonderful opportunity to talk about our families and the game of football. I spent three days with Jason on his NFC sideline and he made me feel like I was part of the family. Thank you, Jason.

During the night of the game, Tracy Perlman and Donovan Darius got me into the NFL Legends Community Lounge in a luxury box with all the former NFL players to watch the Pro-Bowl. It was like a who's who of the NFL Hall of Famers, All-Stars and just scrub NFL players like myself. We all had a great time and enjoyed the hospitality that the NFL showed to us.

That's when the NFL Commissioner of football, Roger Goodell, walked in. Never in a million years would I think Mr. Goodell would be in the same suite that we were all in. He came up to me and Mike Hollis and said, "They allowed kickers in here?" some guys laughed. I answered, "Yes, even NFL Commissioners." We all laughed.

Mr. Goodell is a gracious and kind man. He gave me his full attention as he listened to my suggestions. He could have just walked in and said hello and turned around and walked out. Instead, we talked about the

With NFL Commissioner Roger Goodell and Odell Beckham Jr.

NFL LODP officiating program for the former NFL players who want to someday be working as NFL officials. We agreed about a few ideas and how to make the program stronger and better.

He continued our conversation with suggesting that the VP of Football officiating, Mr. Dean Blandino, should be aware of our conversation. He was giving his full support to the project. I was humbled that Mr. Goodell gave me the opportunity to talk about my ideas to help make it a stronger program for future NFL players. After meeting Mr. Goodell, I realized that a lot of players had gotten him wrong. I respect his commitment to make the NFL a family brand. He protects the image and the integrity of the game. As the head of the most popular sport in the USA, he has proven to be a true leader.

The week after the Super Bowl, Tracy Perlman from the NFL called me and suggested that I write an email to Dean Blandino. You see, if someone told me that I would be talking to Dean Blandino about the future of NFL officiating, I would have told them that they were crazy. Then again, Why not? I had asked the Universe for this and it happened. I remember saying to my wife, not so long ago, that someday, "I'm going to meet Roger Goodell and thank him for the opportunity he has given to former NFL players. I'll explain to him that we should recruit the best former NFL players and the best Division I Football players and teach them how to be great officials. This is the narrative I had been talking about with Wally Hough and Tony Mahalik for the past several months.

Dean Blandino did call me and we had the most productive and promising conversation about the NFL LODP program and several other ideas to help create more opportunities for future football officials. I highly respect Dean and appreciated his time. Dean has changed the way football fans perceive officials. He was clever to challenge fans to make the call. This is a man who understands people and he is a great listener. My grandfather would say "The smart man will listen; a dumb man likes to hear himself speak." Dean is a very smart man and I truly respect his business sense.

Since the writing of this book, Dean resigned his position with the NFL. He is now perusing a career in television. My only hope and 'ask' right now, is that the NFL continues the program and makes it stronger for future generations of former NFL players. I am so passionate about officiating and making this program work for future NFL candidates. That would be a dream come true to someday work for the NFL and build up this program.

With my friend Darryl Talley at the NFL Pro Bowl 2017.

Finally-- I Finished My Children's Books!

Recently my family and I were driving home from Walt Disney World. It sounds like a huge adventure, but we only live 20 minutes away from the Magic Kingdom Theme Park. During our ride, I was having a conversation with Colleen about what I should do for my next work project. Our son Nathaniel loves to listen to our conversations like it was the hottest news off the press. Nate shouted out, "Finish your children's books." Colleen and I looked at each other, then I turned and smiled back at him and said, "You really like my books, huh?" Our other son Mikey replied, "You have the coolest books ever Dad, everyone at my old school loved to read them. Our librarian would never allow anyone to take them out because they were so popular."

Snowyville - A Christmas Experience

Twin Treasures- A pirate treasure hunt

Some of the greatest ideas come out of the mouths of babes. I thanked my sons and Colleen for having so much confidence in me. I explained to them that when I first created the books, they were supposed to be used as storyboard bibles for my animated film projects. They were never intended for commercial use. I would have to work on formatting the books in order to be able to sell them on Amazon.

That night I was so motivated and touched by my son's words that I reviewed my old files and decided to start working on three of my four children's books. I went on the Amazon site and got as much information as possible to start publishing the books. I had to make several rewrites and correct most of the artwork to fit into a children's genre.

You must be careful when you're creating children's books because you need to be conscience about your young readers. Are they engaged? Are

Zandora - An explorer adventure Cereal- An epic journey

you teaching a lesson? Are you appealing to their likes of artwork? Many factors go into writing a children's book and you do not want to rush the process. In fact, it took me several months to create the new artwork and story text to work as a complete children's book.

All three of my children's books can be found on Amazon.com. I am so proud of these children's books because they were inspired by my children. I am still working on the fourth book. My sons now understand how the creative process works and that you can never rush any piece of art if it is to be done right.

The Social Black Belt Project

One of my dearest friends, Dominic Ambrosio, reached out to me about a new project that he is involved in. It's called the Social Black Belt. I had met Dr. Chris and Stephanie Cortman in 2016. This power couple developed and designed this incredible social educational program for children. The Cortman's life's work inspired me to get involved in the project and I signed on as a consultant. I vetted the company for several months.

Then I decided to jump into the everyday workings of a new company. As you know, startups take a lot of time and work before they begin turning a profit. My inspiration was my own children. The thought that I could help them learn how to strengthen their social skills motivated me. This business plan was different. It has been proven to help children learn social skills that will make them better human beings. The Cortmans implicated their educational curriculum in Sarasota County, Florida. The Cortman's program has had a huge effect on over 6000 students.

With NFL Commissioner Roger Goodell, Dr. Chris Cortman
and Former Tampa Bay All-Pro Clifton Smith

It was clear why Dominic asked me to become involved with the Social Black Belt. He knew the program needed a well-known business partner in the national market. If the NFL Alumni logo and branding was attached, it would bring instant credibility to their program.

As a former chapter president of the NFL Alumni, I understood and identified with dozens of former NFL players who needed the opportunity of a job. I had to put together the right team to take this to the next level. I've worked with teams all my life and this was not an uncharted territory for me. In fact, I thrive on putting together the art of the deal.

I turned to my old friend and former superintendent of schools at Long Branch, Joseph Ferraina, for his experience and leadership. Joseph set up several successful meetings with a few superintendents of schools in the Monmouth County area. They all wanted the Social Black Belt program in their school district.

Stephanie Cortman, Dr. Chris Cortman, Hall of Fame-Larry and Rosie Little

In a few months, we worked out the details between Social Black Belt and the NFL Alumni. We made a presentation to NFL Alumni National. Our goal was to create jobs for former NFL players who were looking for new opportunities. In return, the NFL Alumni brand would immediately legitimize the Social Black Belt program on our national marketing plan.

Once we had the attention of the NFL Alumni, I advised Dominic to come with me to Washington, DC. Then we met with a longtime friend, lobbyist and attorney by the name of Bert Peña. Bert and I were introduced by my sister Francine at the Spring Lake Bath and Tennis Club in New Jersey. It only took one dinner for Bert and me to see that we had a lot in common. I pitched Bert the concept of Social Black Belt. He then agreed to represent the Cortman's company pro bono at his law firm. A kind gesture that I will always be grateful for.

Bert and I set up several key meetings in Washington, DC with Senator Marco Rubio, Senator Cory Booker, Congressman Frank Pallone and Congresswoman Virginia Foxx who was the Chairwoman for the Congressional Education Committee.

My goal was to help take this program out to the nation. It would give every child the opportunity to learn social life skills. The goal of the skills is to mold our current generation of children into strong future leaders. This social educational program will not only help my children, but your children as well. That is why I became so passionate about taking their program on the national level. We started to hire NFL players to help teach the program. They worked with local educators. The response level from the students took it to another positive level.

The Social Black Belt program will one day be a household name. It will happen because of government leaders who were not afraid of change. The greatest gifts that we can give every child is an education and the ability to live and communicate with their peers in peace.

My Family
The Greatest Summer Ever

The Attardi Clan in Washington, DC

When I look back to all the wonderful travels our family has shared, one summer takes the prize. It was the summer of 2014, Matthew was already 1-year old and we decided to go back to New Jersey to see our family and friends. We choose to take the Amtrak auto-train from Sanford, Florida to Lorton, Virginia.

We stopped over in Washington, D.C. because our oldest son, Mikey, was being honored by several Senators and Congressmen for what he did for the victims of Super Storm Sandy in 2012. Mikey was honored with the Boy Scout Medal of Merit and a Congressional Citation for bravery. Now I understood how my father felt when I received an award.

We also went to visit all the museums and monuments at the National Mall. Colleen and I thought it was important for our sons to learn about America and our unique government. We toured the Capitol, House of Representatives and Senate buildings. This trip allowed me to teach my children what my father had taught me. Colleen and I also learned so much about our country on that trip.

The Lincoln Memorial and National Harbor in Maryland

When we arrived in New Jersey, the first place I wanted to see again was Fort Hancock on Sandy Hook. I showed my children the same buildings and homes that both my grandfathers had helped construct during WWII. The boys had a blast as we climbed up the oldest lighthouse in America.

Sandy Hook Lighthouse in New Jersey

That summer, we went to the beach every day and explored the Jersey Shore. We went crabbing for blue claws, fishing, surfing, snorkeling,

These are the buildings at Fort Hancock that both my grandfathers
took part in the construction of during World War II

shell hunting and we body surfed the Jersey Shore waves. My sons were
experiencing the same life experiences that I had as a young boy growing
up on the Jersey Shore. Maybe that is why it was one of my greatest
summers ever. I was teaching my sons for the first time how it was to grow
up on the shore. How to explore, how to ask questions, how to invent, how
to fail at something and succeed the second time. We were creative and we
enjoyed our time as a family.

Our Family- Michael, Colleen, Matthew, Mikey, and Nathaniel

What Mom Used to Say

My mother with our sons Mikey, Nate and Matthew

I remember things that happened when I was seven years old. The many memories of my past were great! Thinking back over fifty years ago, I've learned to know many wonderful things.

My Mother was gentle, she was fair and strong. She was always for RIGHT and never for WRONG! She had all these catch phases she used to say, that must have been very popular back in her day. I would love to share with you, these words of WIT. I can't believe I'm still alive today after I gave my Mom all that S_T!

What my Mom used to say and how I responded.

Ages 7-12

Mom- Close the door! You don't live in a barn.
Me- What if we did live in a barn, Mom? What would you say then? Close the door! We don't live in a house? You call us animals anyway!

Mom- Do you think I'm made of money?

Me- If you were made out of money, I would have had Dad feed you more and make you fatter!

Mom- Don't pick your nose in public.
Me- Can I pick it at home in private? (Hits my hand) What? What'd I say?

Mom- Don't sit too close to the television, it'll ruin your eyes.
Me- Is that what happened to you, I'm five feet away?

Mom- Don't talk with your mouth full!
Me- Then how can I talk to you when I'm eating and you're asking me what I learned in school today? (The stare down) What'd I say?

Mom- Don't walk away when I'm talking to you!
Me- I wasn't walking, I was skipping Mom!

Mom- Eat your vegetables, they're good for you.
Me- Except for CORN Mom. Corn and I don't agree. Ask Dad, it doesn't agree with him either.

Mom- Beds are NOT made for jumping on.
Me- Then why do they have bouncy springs in them, Mom?

Ages 14-16

Mom- All I do is follow you around like a dog, picking up after you like some kind of maid.
Me- You've got me confused. Are you a dog or are you a maid? (Smack) What, What'd I say?

Mom- Are you deaf or something?
Me- No, but I stutter! Does that count? What, What'd I say?

Mom- Are you lying to me? You know God is watching you right now. I'm gonna ask you one last time, who ate the Chocolate Chip Cookies Michael?
Me- Mom, why would God be watching me? Were they his Chocolate Chip Cookies? If so, Francine ate them.

Mom- As long as you live under my roof, you'll do as I say.
Me- Ok fine Mom, can you make me my grilled cheese
sandwich now?

Ages 17-20

Mom- Going to a party? Leave a phone number in case I need to
call you.
Me- Ok, 867-5309. She never got that joke. In fact, I think she
called it one time.

Mom- Going to a party? Will their parents be home?
Me- Of course, who do you think is buying the beer, Mom?
Only kidding!

Mom- I brought you into this world, and I can take you right
back out!
Me- I know when to quit Mom! I'll shut up.

Mom- I hope someday you have children just like you.
Me- Me too, Handsome, Smart, Funny. Should I keep going?

Mom- You just ate an hour ago!
Me- Are you timing me?

Mom- I just want what's best for you.
Me- Mom, a white tuxedo with turquoise ruffles, is not a game
changer. In fact, I'll kick my own ass if I wear this to the prom!

Ages 21-30

Mom- I'm not going to ask you again.
Me- I'm sorry, did you say something? (smack) I'm only
kidding!

Mom- I'm not your cleaning lady!
Me- If you were, I would fire you for bleaching my shirt.

Mom- I'm not your waitress!

Me- But Mom, you're the best cook in the world! (Silence)
Really! (She Smiles)

Mom- Look at me when I'm talking to you.
Me- I was. You just can't see my eyes behind my sunglasses.

Mom- No child of MINE would do something like that?
Me- I thought you said that I was adopted? (Laughter)

Ages 30 – Present

Mom- People in HELL are asking for cold water as well.
Me- Come on Mom, can you please loan me $500!

Mom- When I was a little girl...
Me- I know, you had to walk ten miles in the snow with no
shoes on as a grizzly bear chased you. It was hell back then,
Huh? (Silence) What, What'd I say?

Mom- Where do YOU think you're going?
Me- To Hawaii! Do you want to come? I'm not kidding, you're
going to Hawaii! I bought your ticket already! Start packing!
(Silence)

Mom- You don't always get what you want. It's a hard lesson,
but you might as well learn it now.
Me- I was thinking after 50 years of hearing that, I would be
able to reverse the curse, somehow! It's not going to happen, is
it?

Mom- You have an answer for everything, don't you?
Me- If you look up the word Wikipedia on the internet, my
picture is next to it! I'm not kidding. Google, it! (Mom starts to
dance) Mom, Stop that! Google is not the new dance craze.

Mom- You kids are trying to drive me crazy!
Me- I thought we already did years ago!

Mom- You never marry the one you can live with, you marry the
one you can't live without!

Me- How TRUE!

Mom- You'll understand when you're older.
Me- Mom, I do understand.

Mom, I understand that you brought us joy when we were sad. Smiles when we were mad. You kept us warm when we were cold. When we were shy, you made us bold. You made us safe when we were scared. You made us brush our teeth and comb our hair. When we were weak, you made us strong. You taught us right instead of wrong. You inspire us, you made us dream. You've taken us places, we've never seen. A simple thank you is not enough. Or something from Macy's or material stuff.

The only gift that can be given you see. Was sent by god many years ago, my father, my sisters and me. God bless our Mother, your sister, your aunt, your cousin, your grandmother but most of all, your friend!

I love you so much. "From here to the Moon and BACK!"

My Three Sons

Mikey, Colleen, Matty and Nate

One of the greatest gifts that God has bestowed on me is my family. Starting with how I was raised by my parents to being blessed with children of my own. Words can never be used to explain the love and respect that I have for my family. In the last 14 years, God has blessed Colleen and me with three healthy and beautiful sons.

During the writing of this book, Michael Jr. who everyone calls "Mikey" has turned fourteen years old, Nathaniel who is nicknamed "Nate" by his friends, just turned eleven. Our third addition Matthew, "Matty," turned four years old. They are all so different with their own personalities that make Colleen and me laugh. We have so many stories that we can tell about each one; it was hard to pick only these few stories to share with you. It is amazing to see how their minds work and how they process things. That is what makes parenting fun.

Our first son Mikey is one of those intelligent book smart kids. Everyone in school looks to him when they can't answer a question from the teacher. He's also the one who would whisper the answer so a friend would not get caught being stumped. He's a first degree Black Belt and up for his Eagle rank in Boy Scouts. People say he's an overachiever, I say he's driven by his own dreams.

When Mikey was around five years old I took him to Spring Lake, New Jersey to walk around their beautiful lake. Mikey loves animals and I knew that Spring Lake had several large white swans and many ducks. I decided to teach him about caring for animals and took him to feed the ducks and fish with bread.

When we arrived at the lake, three dozen ducks surrounded us and Mikey started to throw bread to them. I then showed him that if he held out his hand, the ducks would eat the bread right off his palm. Mikey then bent down and was about to pick up a piece of duck poo. I ran over to him before he touched the duck poo and said. "No Mikey! Don't touch that. It's dirty!" Mikey replied, "Why not Daddy?" I said, "You should never touch that. That's duck poo. It's like when you do poo-poo in the potty, the ducks do poo-poo on the ground." Mikey understood and stayed clear of any duck poo, although he pointed it out every time he saw some. After a few hours of feeding the animals, we drove home. Spring Lake is around a thirty-minute drive from our house in Middletown.

A few weeks went by and I was working in my office. I was on a conference call with an investor of mine. Mikey came running into my office shouting that I needed to come with him and it was important. I excused myself from the call thinking that something was wrong with Colleen. I ran downstairs and Mikey was already out the backdoor and on our deck. Now, I was shouting for Colleen to see if she was alright. Colleen was standing there with a smile on her face. I said, "Are you alright? Colleen replied, "I'm great. Just wait until you hear this one." Mikey grabbed my hand and pulled me to the other side of our deck. Mikey pointed to the deck and said, "Look Dad, duck poo!" Mikey was right. A duck had pooed on our deck. Colleen said, "Tell Daddy what you told me." Once again, Colleen was smiling. Mikey said, "Can you believe that that duck flew all the way from Spring Lake to do poo-poo on our deck?"

Our second son Nathaniel is brilliant. He's more of a street-smart kid who is very creative and innovative. Nathaniel is my father reincarnated. I am not kidding! He is well past his years in maturity and has the best one-liners ever. Like my father, Nate can be stealth in a room until the party breaks out. Then Nate is the rising star with his witty humor and reserved personality. He's the only one of my sons that gets me to laugh when I am reprimanding him, because he is laughing out of fear. He has an incredible sense of humor and knows how to make people around him feel important. Nathaniel is a diamond in the rough.

During the presidential elections in 2012, my son Mikey asked what the Bill of Rights were. He also wanted to know what is self-reliance? He asked me these questions while we were at the dinner table. We were waiting for Colleen who was cooking my mother's famous meatball recipe. For the record, Colleen's meatballs and tomato gravy is incredible.

I went on to explain to my sons the Bill of Rights in simple terms for a ten and seven-year-old to understand. I started to talk about self-reliance. I said, "Everything we have in this house was paid for with money that Mommy and Daddy had earned. I go to work every day and get paid money for my job. I take that money and give it to Mommy to buy food, pay bills and buy things that sometimes you boys ask for. I don't get money handed to me for free. If I were sick or couldn't work then the government would try and help.

The secret is to save your money so you will not have to ask for help. For example, the food that Mommy is cooking is not free. We had to pay for it. People used to have to hunt and grow their own food before we had grocery stores. We can now go to a store and buy everything we need. The advancement of technology and food distribution has made that possible. However, everything cost money.

At that moment Colleen handed me the bowl of her famous meatballs to dish out. Mikey and Nate's eyes grew wider with excitement. I placed a meatball on Mikey's plate and said, "That will cost you a dollar." Mikey smiled at me and said, "Come on Dad, give me another one." I placed a second meatball on his plate and said, "That will now cost you two dollars." I placed a meatball on Nate's plate and turned back to Mikey. I gave him a stern look as if I were dead serious. Mikey looked at me and looked back at the ? eaten meatball and began to cry. With tears running down his face he said, "When did you start charging for food around here?"

Colleen is kicking me under the table to stop harassing our sons. I answered Mikey and said, "That is what I'm trying to teach you. Nothing is for free. Did you clean your room today? Did you take out the garbage? Did you help your mother clean the dishes? Did you do anything today that would warrant me to give you these meatballs?" Mikey said, "No."

Nate started to laugh with his mouth half filled with a meatball. I turned to Nate and said, "What about you, Mister? What do you have to say for yourself?" Nate looked down at his plate. Then he looked at me with serious eyes and said, "I only ate fifty-cents worth. That's all I'm going to pay." Nate pulled a dollar from out of his pocket and placed it on the table. Nate then said, "I expect my change." I had to leave the room very quickly before my sons noticed that I could not control my laughter. My excuse was that I had to go to the bathroom. Colleen could not stop laughing. It was the funniest thing we ever witnessed as parents. I'm sure we can expect more of that in the future.

Our son Matthew has a special gift of making you happy when you are sad. He looks into your eyes as if he's communicating with your soul. At the age of three, Matthew can work an iPad and Xbox better than most adults can. He reminds me of me. The only advantage that he has, are two wonderful brothers who love and teach him how to be a respectful young man. Matthew has a speech delay. He is in pre-school and is doing incredible. One of the greatest gifts that Matthew has is making us happy if we were sad. He's an affectionate and sweet young man who always wants us to be happy. We expect big adventures with Matthew.

I've shared my life story with you in hopes that I can inspire you to be the best person you can be. My life was not without pain, loss or deception. No one is perfect! No one has a flawless life! No one has all the answers! We were put on this earth by our Creator, to help each other, to teach, to protect, to be kind and to love one another. Everybody has lost something they have loved. Everybody has had a disappointment sometime in their life. If you think you haven't, then you never lived, you never cried and you never lost a loved one.

My Mother with Nate, Mikey and Matty and me

After all my experiences throughout my life, it all brings me back to the most important thing and that's family. My family is everything to me. I cherish them, I live for them and I'm honored and blessed to have them all in my life. My wife Colleen, my sons Michael Jr, Nathaniel and Matthew, my mother, two sisters, my nephew James. They are the reason I fight, sweat and shed tears. I love them all so much. My godchild Noelle and my family and friends.

The secret of life is to embrace your flaws and correct them for another day. The secret of life is to embrace other people's flaws and help make them aware. The secret of life is to be who you are and not what others want you to be. The secret of life is inside of all of us, you just have to find it. May God bless you with health, love and happiness. You all deserve it!

Honored by Two Presidents

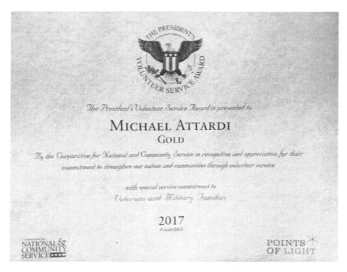

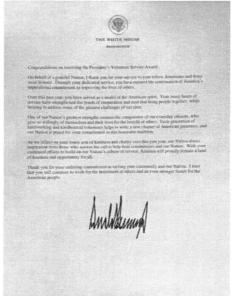

When you're a little boy growing up in the 1970's, the world around you appears to be huge. I was fortunate to have parents who wanted me to learn about the world. They encouraged me to watch the news on television. I enjoyed learning about local, national and international events. That is one of the reasons that motivated me to own and publish two sports publications. I love media.

I remember watching Richard Nixon's resignation speech on August 8, 1974. Watergate had cost President Nixon much of his political support. He faced almost certain impeachment and removal from the Oval office. Nixon was known as a great political strategist. But, he was one of the unlucky politicians that got caught. I have read several books about him and his relationship with President John F. Kennedy.

I fell in love with politics at an early age. I saw the honor in serving my fellow American. To be a public servant requires many attributes. Public servants should show respect, compromise, determination and fairness to all. My father would say, "You can only make people happy, half of the time." I never agreed with that statement because I am an optimist, always looking at the glass half filled. I look at an issue and propose several solutions, rather than finger pointing.

I spent a few years in Washington, DC During that time I worked on Capitol Hill. The experience was the benchmark and learning grounds for me. I enjoyed the thought of public service. I wanted to have the resources to help empower the less fortunate. I believe that the goal of every public servant. Public service is not a right, it's a responsibility and honor. Those that are in public service should never treat their position as an entitlement. Their role and actions should be one of service for the people, by the people. I have always been a true patriot of freedom. That was instilled at a young age by my parents. I also believe that politicians should be grateful and humbled to serve.

I have worked on many political campaigns. From local elections to state and federal. I have met many Congressmen and Senators who started with these same ideals. It shouldn't matter if you're a Republican, Democrat, Conservative, Liberal or in the middle like me. You need to be able to listen and respect people.

I had a failed city council race in Long Branch, New Jersey. After that, I promised my wife that I would never enter the political arena again. I kept this promise for over 20 years. I understand that she wants to be private and not draw attention to our core family. I respect that and that is why I have not run for a public office. Even though many others said I should. Instead, I went into philanthropy and raising up my local community.

The theory of the saying that 'it will take a village to raise a child,' worked on me. My book about my life is living proof. What comes to you should be shared with the world. Don't get me wrong, we still talk politics in our family. It's healthy to debate and know the current affairs. We all have different opinions and that is what makes it fun. It would be boring if everyone agreed on every issue. That is why I love democracy.

When I started my charity work, I never looked at it as a personal recognition. It was never supposed to be about me or my family. It was always about helping the children who lived in my community. It was about doing the right and decent things in life for others. It was about teaching my children that another life does matters. No matter what race, creed, color or religion. Colleen and I have taught our children that life is not easy. With that said, we have donated our time and resources to make our community a little bit better.

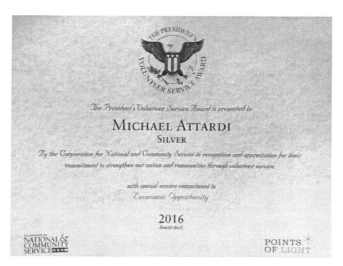

In 2016, I was presented the President's Volunteer Service Award by President Obama. It was an honor that I never expected nor thought that I deserved. I do what I do for people because I care for humanity. I received these award because many local charities had recorded my charity hours and then submitted them for these awards.

I look at my public service as a glass half filled. Although I'm not a Mayor, Congressman or a Senator, I have worked with many people who are. Most of them are great human beings wanting to help make a positive difference for mankind. i look for the good in people and that is why, I do, what I do for charity. When I take on any project, I give it 120% of my time and efforts. When I join a cause, many people say, "You Can't Do That! I say, Yes I Can!"

Curtain Call

I look back at my life and often recall one conversation with my mother and father. It was a defining moment in my life. The two people that I loved and relied on the most were my mother and father before I created my own family. My parents shared with me the Secret of Life. People always thank their mothers and fathers, when they win an award or a special accolade.

My thank you to my parents, comes from my heart with true admiration and understanding for them. They always had the right intentions to teach and guide me. I look back at that time when my father was on his deathbed at the hospital. He turned to me and said that I should be telling my stories. I looked over to my mother, who smiled and nodded her head without saying a single word. That's when I knew that I had to make a change in my life. My mother and I never talked about that conversation. She knew in her heart, that I was going to do whatever they asked of me.

If it wasn't for my wife, and all the support that she gave me throughout the years, I wouldn't be half the man that I am today. Colleen understood that I didn't have war medals to place in my father's coffin. I didn't feel that I had anything of value to put in his coffin. But, what I did have, was an "ask" from my father to me. His "ask" was for me to be the greatest father to my sons, the greatest husband to my wife, the greatest son to my mother, the greatest grandson to my grandparents, the greatest brother to my sisters and the greatest friend to mankind.

With all that I have mentioned, I feel that I've been able to give my father the greatest gift of all. I created a legacy, to leave a legacy. If a person can live on after they have died, then that person was a great human being. My father lives on inside of me and now lives on in my three sons. That's why I needed to tell my stories. My father was a very wise man. I hope someday that by telling my story, that my sons will create their own. Who knows, maybe this book will also inspire you to someday leave your own legacy?

You have dreams within you. The more you use the Law of Attraction, the more you will draw positive power to you. Your own legacy will only grow if you nurture it, like planting a seed. When you build your story, it will give you the power to teach you many things. It will teach you how to be patient, how to strive for perfection, how to be wiser, how to be happier, how to be smarter, and how to love.

The sun will rise for you tomorrow and it will also set. Everything beautiful is for you to see, everything incredible in the world is for you to have. No matter who or what you thought you were before, you were made to accomplish greater things. Look deeper into who you are and that will help make you the most powerful person you can be. Reach for your dreams today and make them into reality tomorrow.

I've learned that my journey through life was not about collecting material things or making money. It's about creating happiness for the people I love and even for the people I have never met before. Some people say that because I just turned 50 years old that I'm halfway there. They're not even close, I haven't even started my life. I have so much more that I want to achieve here on Earth.

I challenge you to use the Laws of Attraction and ask the universe and GOD for what you want. Only then will you be able to leave a legacy of your own.

Life is one exciting ride and I don't ever want it to end!

God Bless!

- Michael

Afterword by Steve Ortmayer

Former General Manager of the Los Angeles Raiders and St. Louis Rams

With my great friend Steve Ortmayer

In 1972 life changed for a little boy growing up in Long Branch, New Jersey. Until then he had lived life within family constraints of tradition, love and the normal experiences of living. Endless possibilities were the spice that made waking up early each day a treat to be shared with sisters, friends and the adults who touched Michael Attardi's life.

Then, in his fifth year he went to have surgery to remove his tonsils. He came away a changed boy with a speech impediment not there before he went under the anesthesia. What was a world of endless possibilities suddenly became cautious adults saying "No, you really can't do that." People expected Mike to accept the fact his impediment would put limits on what his very active mind could realize and accomplish.

This was the beginning of the "Focus" that has guided Mike Attardi. Who knows whether the focus trait was unusually intense in Michael because it was in his genes or whether the speech impediment magnified its presence. Either way it has been the constant in propelling Mike to achieve when he has made the decision to proceed.

Though Michael has led a very full and exciting life, three aspects stand out. The first in chronology is his passion for the performing arts. From the first guidance counselor Mike encountered in high school who told him he would "never go to college" because of his speech impediment, to the taunts of his peers when he wanted to audition for the school play, the world seemed to be telling Mike "You can't do that!". In actuality, now the challenge was ON! Not only did he win the part of the Tin Man in The Wiz but he went on to perform in countless musical productions on the East Coast. Michael had learned that singing songs and memorizing dialog slowed down his thought process so that it didn't surpass his speech process. Thus, a rewarding musical career opened up.

The Second aspect of achievement (and the most pervasive) is Michael's love affair with football. Once again, this endeavor began with adults telling Mike "You can't do that," you only weigh 145 pounds. With a prodigious work ethic, focus and fortuitous encounters with talented mentors, Mike put the doubters to rest. He not only played but captained both high school and collegiate teams. In keeping with his shoot for the moon dedication he landed on a National Football League roster during training camp with the Los Angeles Raiders. The NFL Players Association opened many football doors for Mike and led him to serve in NFL Alumni positions and to his current position in a League sponsored NFL officiating program for future referees and football officials.

Leading to the third and most significant of Michael's remarkable achievements was his encounter at eight years old with Marc Davis, one of the original Disney "Nine Old Men". Mr. Davis fashioned a drawing of Mickey Mouse and personalized it for the young boy from New Jersey. Thirty years later Mike had the opportunity to again meet with Marc Davis who not only remembered him but rekindled Mike's fascination with Disney and animation. The second encounter with the Disney animator led to Michael putting together his own production company in collaboration with Dani Donadi, a conceptual musical composer for Disney. The two men started work on several film projects that culminated in an animated short film, Once Upon A Christmas that won 96 awards including one at the Cannes Film Festival in its category. Once Upon A Christmas became the most successful independently produced short animated film of all time.

This Renaissance entrepreneur has led a very full life. He has experienced great highs and lows. He has managed to cheat death on more than one occasion as chronicled in this honest autobiography. The rollercoaster ride has spanned 50 years. With the love and support of his parents, family, and especially his wife Colleen, Michael has created a life of unending adventure. From playing in the NFL with the L.A. Raiders; 18 holes in one on the golf course; to working on Capitol Hill in D.C.; to singing at The Bitter End, a club in New York City; to editing a couple of newspapers; it seems like more than one life story. But, at the age of fifty, Michael swears that he is just getting started.

Afterword by Michael Broggie

Award Winning Author of Walt Disney's Railroad Story

Upon my first meeting with Michael Attardi, I discovered that we had several interests in common: An unlimited admiration of Walt Disney; a respect for the Imagineering team and their many creations; a passion for classic Disney productions; and, reverence for Walt's "Nine Old Men," who were responsible for producing a remarkable body of hand-crafted art that is regarded as the gold standard of motion pictures we know and love as animated film.

The last survivor of Walt's nine animation legends was Ollie Johnston. It was at a special celebration of his life at a restored theatre on Hollywood Boulevard that I met Michael. I was one of several presenters that afternoon and reflected upon the close connection between Ollie and his mentor, Walt Disney. Among those connections was their shared passion for steam railroading. Ollie introduced Walt to miniature scale steam trains at his home in La Cañada-Flintridge, California. That evolved into Walt's own meticulously crafted one-eighth scale Carolwood Pacific Railroad at his home on Carolwood Drive in the Holmby Hills neighborhood of west Los Angeles. Beyond the backyard pike, Walt's enthusiasm for steam trains eventually grew into Disneyland and a population of themed amusement parks around the world.

In a way, Michael Attardi is a scale model of Walt. He has the same combination of curiosity, confidence, courage and constancy, which are the four Cs I learned directly from Walt as a 12-year-old accompanying him in the cab of the E. P. Ripley on his first steam-up and run at Disneyland a month before the Park opened to the public in 1955. Here, I have to admit, being the son of Walt's first Imagineer, Roger Broggie had its benefits.

Walt taught me to apply these powerful C words to my goals, dreams and visions as he had done to his. Michael seems to have mastered this formula for success as readers of this accounting of his life experiences will learn and appreciate. There are many twists and turns in his saga that will leave fellow travelers with a sense of amazement. How, in a brief half-century, could one individual accomplish so much? Not only in variety, but with achievement and peer recognition.

Master Architect Frank Gehry was describing Imagineer Legend John Hench when he wrote "…a great design makes people think, it inspires them, it makes them use their imaginations. John pushes everyone to a higher standard, a standard of excellence." Gehry could just as well been writing about Michael Attardi.

As Ralph Waldo Emerson said, "There are no days in life so memorable as those which vibrate to some shake of the imagination."

As I was writing this foreword, I remembered a comment Walt shared those many decades ago aboard his engine at the Magic Kingdom in Anaheim: "If I leave this world a better place, then my time here will have been worthwhile." My opinion is that Michael will have this thought to comfort him at the end of his journey.